D1603887

STATE LIBRARY
THE UNION
SALEM, OREGON

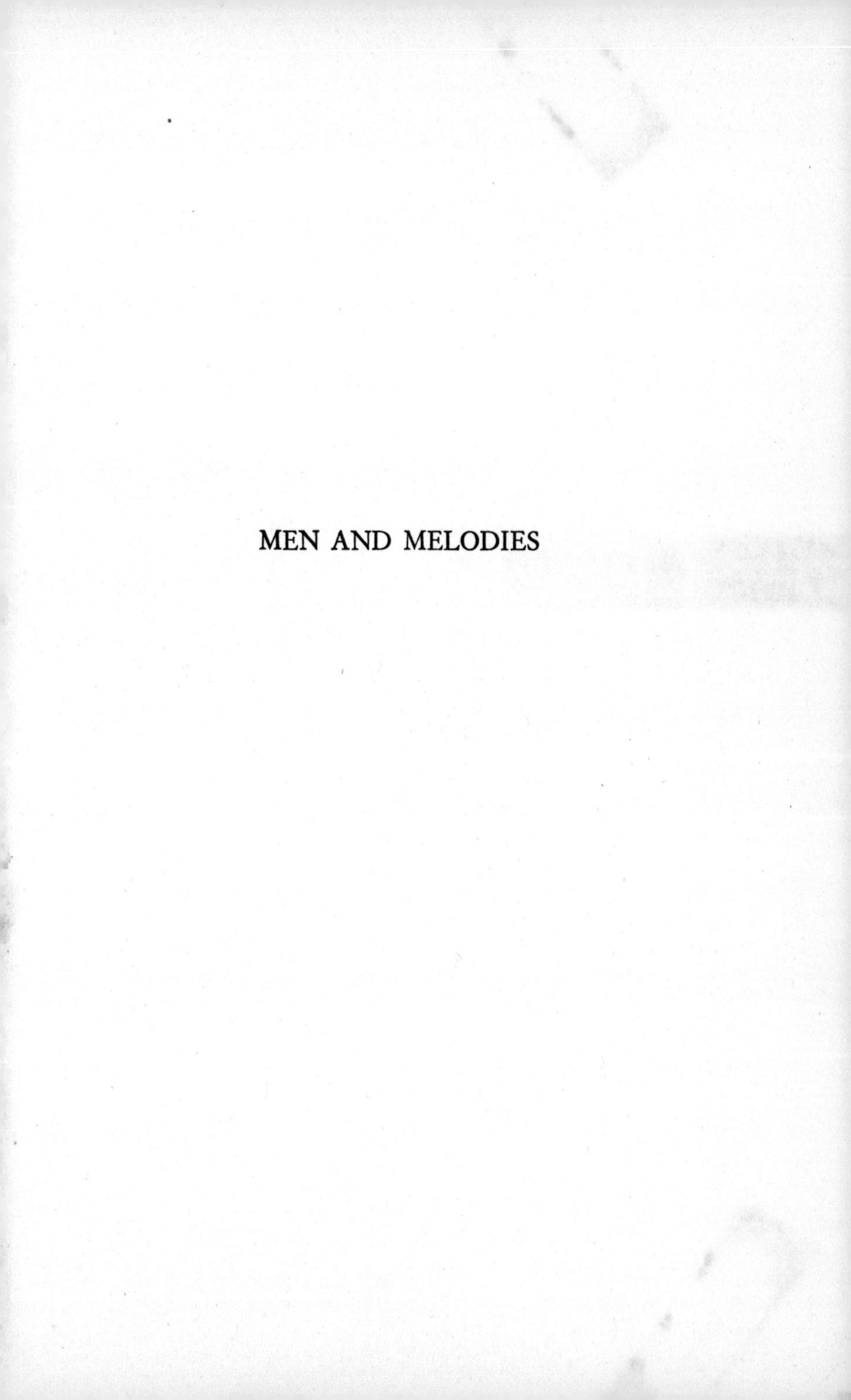

MEN AND MELODIES

MEN *and* MELODIES

Leonard A. Paris

THOMAS Y. CROWELL COMPANY
New York

Manufactured in the United States of America by Vail-Ballou Press, Inc., Binghamton, New York

LIBRARY OF CONGRESS CATALOG CARD NO. 54-9151

First Printing

This book
is dedicated to
MY FATHER
who might have
been part of it

PREFACE

It seemed to me when I began this work that I had a not too formidable task ahead of me. I was simply going to write down some of the facts—and some of the legends—about the men behind the songs you sing.

But I had no sooner begun my labors than the picture darkened. Who *are* the men behind the songs you sing? It was necessary at once to draw some rather fine lines, with which readers of this book may feel free to disagree.

To begin with, I decided to concern myself only with those popular songs which have lasted (and which give promise of lasting) beyond their own time. But I still had a body of work so enormous as to be unwieldy.

More decisions had to be made. I decided to narrow the field to songs of musical comedy and operetta, and to include only those men whose contributions were so consistently outstanding, or so historically significant, that they could not be ignored.

Finally, because of limitations of space, I could write about only the highlights of each man's life, leaving the long periods of placid but productive labor merely to be guessed at.

One of the real joys of writing a book like this is meeting the stimulating people of the theater and of music. To all of those who gave of their time and knowledge, I should like to say "Thanks," but especially to:

Mrs. Ella Stevens Bartlett, for invaluable guidance on the story of her father, Victor Herbert.

Otto Harbach and Oscar Hammerstein II for their illuminating comments on some of the composers with whom they worked.

Mike Todd, Ed Wynn, Peggy Wood, and the late Fritzi Scheff for personal anecdotes.

Edna Ferber, for gracious permission to quote at length from her autobiography, *A Peculiar Treasure* (Doubleday and Company).

Daniel I. McNamara, of the American Society of Composers, Authors and Publishers (ASCAP), whose help extended even beyond *The ASCAP Biographical Dictionary,* which he edited.

And finally, all those day-by-day chroniclers in the newspapers and magazines of the past fifty years.

At my elbow as I worked were two fine reference volumes: Cecil Smith's *Musical Comedy in America,* published in 1950 by Theatre Arts Books; and J. Walker McSpadden's *Operas and Musical Comedies,* published in 1946 by the publishers of this volume.

My chief listener, critic, and assistant while I worked on this book was my wife. Her patience, always greater than mine, proved a real bulwark during long months of research and writing. I owe her more than thanks, for I could not have finished the book without her.

L.A.P.

February, 1954

Contents

Reginald De Koven

HALF a century ago the sight of a tall, monocled man wearing an opera cloak and carrying a walking stick was more common than it is today. But even then, Reginald De Koven was a striking figure. Every inch a gentleman, he customarily looked as though his evening clothes grew on him.

His enemies regarded him as a snob. Even his friends found him somewhat aloof. Yet Reginald De Koven wrote one of the most popular songs ever composed by an American—a song that has been sung by people of every social rank and economic level, and which is still sung today. The song is "Oh, Promise Me," and it is as vital a part of many bridal ceremonies as Mendelssohn's Wedding March.

It was said of De Koven that "he scored his operettas with the aid of a lorgnette." But for all of that, he found the common touch in the one song which was to make him immortal. Others of his works have been neglected, although they are still heard occasionally. But it is "Oh, Promise Me," with its sentimental, emotional appeal, that the world knows and loves best.

De Koven was an ambitious, conscientious composer. Most of his work is too serious to be classed with musical comedy. But "Oh, Promise Me" was composed in twenty minutes and inserted into the score of a show which was already being performed! The play was *Robin Hood,* probably De Koven's greatest work, and certainly one of the most popular and enduring of all American musical plays.

Lest anyone think that De Koven was a musical hack who hit on one lucky number, let us look back at the period in which he lived. It was a period when Victor Herbert was at his best, George M. Cohan was commanding attention, Florenz Ziegfeld and Anna Held were making theatrical history. It was, of course, before the day of the movies, and long before radio and television. Because entertainment was less plentiful than today, those who provided it took time to turn out a superior product. It took talent and determination to stay alive in that kind of competition. De Koven had both.

He was born in Middletown, Connecticut, April 3, 1859. His father was a clergyman and a professor of theology. When young Reginald was eleven, the family moved to Europe because of the elder De Koven's health. Reginald was educated there and took a degree at Oxford. The Oxford accent he acquired stayed with him all his life, as did many of the mannerisms of life on the Continent in the 1880's.

As a matter of fact, Reginald might well have become a member of international society and served no more useful purpose. For, after Oxford, he drifted back to Stuttgart, where he had studied music, piano, and harmony, and then to

Florence. He had many friends, a modest inheritance, and no particular responsibilities. He was still young.

But at the age of twenty-three, he decided it was time he made something of himself. He felt that he would find a purpose in America. So he returned and took a job in Chicago at his uncle's bank.

At this point there had been little indication that the theater was to be his career. He had composed some songs—polite, graceful ditties for the drawing rooms of Europe. But they reflected little of his musical training at Stuttgart, and even less of his flair for the dramatic. At Newport one summer he had scored as an amateur comedian. (He did it by standing on his head in one scene, his wife later reported.) But it wasn't until after his marriage in 1884, and several years of amateur theatricals, that he seriously turned to writing light operas.

Even then, it was only a sideline. His first one, *The Begum,* was produced in 1887, when De Koven was a shipping clerk in a wholesale dry goods house in Chicago. But once he had read the notices—at five o'clock in the morning, after a night of waiting—his course was mapped. The reviews were only fair, but they offered him all the encouragement he needed. More important, the public bought tickets.

Light opera—or comic opera, as it is sometimes called—was not then widely accepted in this country. The few who practiced the art were mostly Europeans, so De Koven's successful entry into the ranks opened up a whole new field for American composers. But he was swimming against the tide, and there were family objections.

He was obligated to his wife's father, Charles B. Farwell, United States Senator from Illinois and a prominent Chicago businessman. Farwell had given the young couple his blessing, sent them on a European honeymoon, and taken Reginald out of the bank and into the J. V. Farwell Company, a wholesale dry goods house.

De Koven's start, as a shipping clerk, was lowly; but he rose rapidly to the credit department, where he devised a credit system that was a great improvement over anything that had existed before. To toss this aside lightly in favor of a career in comic opera must have seemed foolish indeed to Senator Farwell. He voiced his objections, as did Reginald's banker uncle. Music was all right as a diversion, they agreed. But for a life's work—never!

Avoiding an open break, even after the success of *The Begum,* De Koven continued to work in Chicago. But the virus was in his blood, and he was determined to have a musical career. He faced criticism from other quarters as well. Critics and other musicians who were envious of his triumph with *The Begum* said that he was nothing more than a highbrow leader of cotillions—not a serious musician at all. A malicious rumor spread that the music for *The Begum* had actually been written, not by De Koven, but by a German named Seebeck whom De Koven had hired to do some copying. De Koven spiked this rumor by offering to give up all his royalties to anyone who could prove the story. The whispering campaign promptly ceased.

Meanwhile, De Koven continued to aim toward a musical career. In 1888 he and Mrs. De Koven were able to return to Europe for a few months, leaving their young daughter with Mother Farwell. There Reginald studied orchestration with Delibes and other European masters and continued to compose—mostly songs.

In her own autobiography, published in 1925, Mrs. De Koven wrote that when her husband was composing, he never heard a word she spoke to him. At first she was deeply hurt and "wept for three weeks." Finally she gave up and got to work herself—work which was to lead to a writing career. She began in Europe that year by translating a French novel. From then on she was seldom without some literary project—novels, stories, history, biography. By the time of her death in 1953 (she was 92 years old), Anna De Koven had published a respectable shelf of works.

Yet she made her own career secondary to De Koven's. Once she had aspired to sing; but when she heard his song, "Oh, Promise Me," she knew that he was to be the musician in the family.

De Koven's second operetta was *Don Quixote,* which was produced in 1889 after his return to America. It was fairly successful, enough so that he was able to give up his job in Chicago and devote all his time to music.

The next year brought *Robin Hood.* Nothing could have had a more unpretentious start. De Koven had composed the music in three months during the winter of 1888–89. Harry B. Smith, who had supplied the books for De Koven's earlier efforts, wrote this one in three weeks. A light opera company known as the Bostonians agreed to produce the show. They spent all of $109.50 on it. The leading tenor wore a costume left over from *Il Trovatore,* and the rest of the wardrobe and scenery were hand-me-downs from earlier productions. In short, when *Robin Hood* went before the footlights in Chicago that June in 1890, no one expected very much.

What they got was a pleasant, tuneful tale based on the legendary adventures of Robin Hood—something that would probably not win much applause in these days of three dimensional movies and color television. But the charm and beauty of the music and the story arrested the audience that night. They left the theater humming and whistling "Brown October Ale" and the other lively tunes. Later "Oh, Promise Me" added even more luster to the score.

Robin Hood was at once something simple and popular, yet something new to American audiences. It was the first really important comic opera by an American composer. It made the Bostonians; it made Harry B. Smith; it made De Koven. For the next twenty years it was performed continually in one place or another, and De Koven was never without substantial royalties from it.

As a matter of fact, *Robin Hood* became so closely identified with De Koven that he couldn't escape from it. Everything he wrote thereafter was compared with *Robin Hood.* Joe Jefferson, the actor who made a career out of playing "Rip Van Winkle," once told De Koven: "You will never live down *Robin Hood.* I have had to play 'Rip' all my life; the public would not have me in any other role."

De Koven sometimes grew tired of *Robin Hood*'s popularity. Once at a dinner party a young lady who was seated next to him did not realize his identity. "I don't understand all this fuss about *Robin Hood,"* she remarked. "I didn't think much of it."

"Neither do I," De Koven replied. "But then, I wrote it."

De Koven's uncle, the one who had objected to his musical career, had another reason to regret that Reginald had not stuck to the dry goods business. On a business trip to Los Angeles, the uncle was virtually mobbed by *Robin Hood* fans who insisted that he was the De Koven of operetta fame.

In fact, the craze for *Robin Hood* cannot be compared with anything we know today. We idolize movie stars and popular singers, but not composers. Most of the time we don't even know—or care—who they are. The audiences of those days were not nearly so blasé. Unable to turn on their radios and hear the latest popular tunes, they were enormously impressed by the men and women who brought music and excitement into their lives.

Proud as he was to receive this popular acclaim, De Koven was not satisfied. He had not convinced the critics that he was a serious musician. He did not want to be a mere "flash in the pan"—a composer who is known for just one work. So while *Robin Hood* spun on its melodious way around the country and abroad to London, De Koven moved to New York and continued his work. As music critic on the New York *World* he came to know many of the famous personalities of his day—the famed pianist Paderewski, Schumann-Heinck, Melba, Sembrich and other opera stars. They were frequent guests in his home. Although he never asked them to sing at these musical gatherings, the famous guests often did perform.

Once he wanted to hire Woolf and Hollman, the famous violin-cello duo, for a home musicale. They accepted happily but refused to accept any fee from a professional musician. Mrs. De Koven said that he reported this to her with wonder. "Do you think of me as a professional musician?" he wanted to know. This, from the man whose *Robin Hood* had made musical history!

In 1893 De Koven went to Boston to conduct the premiere of his new operetta, *The Algerian*. If he hoped to have another *Robin Hood* on his hands, he was disappointed. The play was, in fact, so bad that the entire audience walked out after the second act.

Discouraged by this failure, De Koven nevertheless began work on another operetta. This was *Rob Roy,* produced successfully in 1894. While it did not have the lasting popularity of *Robin Hood,* it was a respectable recovery after the fiasco of *The Algerian.* In 1897 came *The Highwayman,* which many regard as De Koven's best work.

Twenty years after its premiere, *The Highwayman* was revived in New York, with John Charles Thomas in the leading role. One of the characters in the operetta was a constable named Foxy Quiller. For a number of years around the turn of the century this name came to be slang for a greenhorn who thinks he's smart. You may still hear it once in a while, from some oldster who has clung to the speech of his youth.

At about this time De Koven moved to Washington, where he organized and conducted the Washington Symphony Orchestra. His solid musical training in Europe—particularly in orchestration—suited him for this new work. He was an exacting conductor, insisting on at least six rehearsals before every performance.

The De Kovens remained in Washington six years. Mrs. De Koven became well known as a Washington hostess and her husband found time to continue composing as well as to set down some thoughts about comic opera in general.

"I believe," he wrote at this time, "that the day of comic opera in America has come. I mean genuine comic opera containing the necessary ingredients of humor and music. I hold that Offenbach was just as great a genius as Wagner, and that his music will live as long as the music of Wagner."

These were perhaps bold words for the conductor of a symphony orchestra, but they came from the heart of a man whose popular operettas were already promising to become immortal.

Altogether De Koven wrote nineteen operettas. They ranged all the way from such frothy items as *The Little Duchess,* which was memorable chiefly because of the French charms of Anna Held, to such substantial works as *The Highwayman.* Though few of the songs from these operettas had the lasting appeal of "Oh, Promise Me," critics regard some of the music—particularly that in *The Highwayman*—as better. Unfortunately, little of it is heard today.

In his later years De Koven tried his hand at grand opera, as well. His *The Canterbury Pilgrims* (1917) and *Rip Van Winkle* (1920) were both written in collaboration with the well-known American poet, Percy MacKaye. Although they are not performed today, they were considered successful in their time.

The difficulties De Koven had in getting them staged, however, might have discouraged a lesser man. He wrote the score for *The Canterbury Pilgrims,* based an Chaucer's *The Canterbury Tales,* in Switzerland, while World War I was raging elsewhere in Europe. De Koven had gone abroad to recover his health. (He had hardening of the arteries.) During two years there, he finished the manuscript and started for home.

Journeying by ship in those perilous days was enough to wreck the strongest man's nerves, for the waters were infested by submarines. As a matter of fact, the ship on which De Koven crossed the Channel was later sunk by subs.

He arrived home safely. But his troubles were far from

over. The Metropolitan Opera manager, Gatti Cassazza, had heard the music in Switzerland and Otto Kahn, famed patron of the Met, had commissioned it. But now there were doubts whether an ambitious undertaking of this sort would be wise at this time. De Koven managed to remove the doubts—after much discussion and uncertainty—and the opera opened at the Met on March 8, 1917.

At its third performance, an ominous announcement was made from the stage. The United States had declared war on Germany! The two principal singers, both Germans, fainted. The performance was concluded, but the future of *The Canterbury Pilgrims* was cloudy. German musicians soon became unpopular in a wave of war hysteria, and Gatti refused to reassemble the cast in the face of threats from the public.

De Koven tried to save the opera by organizing a national American opera company, but the war was too much with us. He could not arouse sufficient interest.

During the following year, De Koven failed in health, but rallied enough to start work on *Rip Van Winkle*. In the fall of 1919 he had finished the work and went to Chicago to supervise its production.

Again bad luck plagued him. The man who had commissioned the opera died three weeks before it was to open. The company, worried about salaries and continuing work, began to fall apart. The manager tried to whip them into shape with only six rehearsals. The conductor resigned. Everything went wrong!

Nevertheless, De Koven persisted, and he saw his opera come to life on the stage of the Chicago Opera House in January of 1920. A New York production was arranged for a few weeks later. But in the meantime De Koven had become ill again. He died on the eve of the third performance of his second opera—in Chicago, where he had started his musical career.

After De Koven's death, his wife continued to live in their mansion at 1025 Park Avenue, New York city. The fabulous sixteenth-century music room where he had introduced so many of his own works remained untouched as a memorial to the composer. His silk hat, his sable-lined overcoat, his gold-headed cane—all of these were to be seen just as though laid out by De Koven's own valet. The memorial remained until 1946, when Mrs. De Koven moved to a hotel and the mansion was renovated and converted into apartments.

But old-timers, when they hear "Oh, Promise Me" or "Brown October Ale," recall the dignified, bemonocled composer who never quite succeeded in becoming a serious musician but who still remained a little startled by his own popularity.

VICTOR HERBERT

GREAT men have always been the subject of legends. George Washington and the cherry tree; Robert Bruce and the spider; Abraham Lincoln doing his lessons on a spade. The greater the man, the more legends. As time passes, it becomes more and more difficult to separate truth from fiction.

This is as true in the world of music as in any other field. Think of the stories about the fabled meeting between Beethoven and Schubert; about Mozart's amazing precocity; about Wagner's temper. True or not, these stories have come to be part of a body of legend that spells greatness.

Perhaps they are even a measure of greatness. If so, then Victor Herbert certainly should stand as one of the greatest names in music. For the stories about him are so numerous—and often, so dubious—that it is hard to see the man as he was.

Fortunately we do not have to depend on legend to judge Herbert's greatness. We have a much more reliable gauge in the music which he wrote. It is music which wears well; it is as lovely today as when he wrote it. And it is music which has form and character. Many a hack musician who wrote for the same audience and at the same time as Herbert has been long forgotten, but Victor Herbert will be remembered as long as there are ears to hear his melodies.

On this basis alone, Herbert was one of the great men of music. Add to this the fact that he played an enormous role in the shaping of the whole musical and theatrical era, and the man emerges as a titan. No wonder they told stories about him!

They told stories about his appetite—champagne for breakfast; about his showmanship—he loved the spotlight; about his wit, his generosity, his energy, his temperament. Some of the stories were true, and some were false. But true or false, they were inevitable.

The plain facts of Herbert's life are not especially dramatic. He was born in Ireland, educated in Germany. He came to the United States as a young man to play in the Metropolitan Opera orchestra. Around the turn of the century he started writing for the theater, while continuing more serious composition. His light operas were immediately successful and he devoted most of his time to them from then on. He had a simple, quiet home life with his wife and two children. He died in 1924.

But that is only an outline. And it was perfectly normal for theater folk—the men and women with whom he worked—to fill in the gaps with rich detail. Some years ago, when Hollywood decided to make a movie called *The Great Victor Herbert,* the writers chose to focus all their attention on the fables and legends and very little on the facts. The result was that almost the only true thing in the film was Mary Martin's voice singing some of the great Herbert songs.

Most of his songs are as familiar today as they were forty years ago. "Kiss Me Again," "Ah, Sweet Mystery of Life," "Gypsy Love Song," "March of the Toys"—they recall another time, a slower, more leisurely time, but one which it is pleasant to remember. Herbert has had his turn, too, on the Hit Parade. If there had been such a poll in his day, he certainly would have stood at the top of it. But to have made it years after his death is even more remarkable. He did it with "Indian Summer," a Herbert melody provided with words.

It would have pleased him to know that. He once asked: "Is it a crime to be popular? Personally, I hold that which is not 'popular' is not of much benefit to the world."

This was a theory which underlay much of his work. It does not mean that he wrote only popular music, as we understand that term today. For he also produced orchestral suites, concertos, and other instrumental works, and even grand operas. But it does mean that Victor Herbert was not afraid to write melodies that people could hum and whistle and sing.

His mother, who was an accomplished pianist, used to sing old Irish tunes to him as a baby, and it is said that Victor could sing them himself before he could talk. Music, therefore, was among his earliest memories.

Born in Dublin in 1859, he spent a great part of his boyhood in the home of his grandfather, Samuel Lover. Lover was an Irish patriot and man of the arts. Through his daughter, who was Victor Herbert's mother, he passed along to the boy a love of music, good taste, a sense of the dramatic, and a passion for lively talk. None of these attributes was ever to desert Victor.

His father had died when he was quite young, and when

it came time for Victor to be educated, it was natural that his mother should turn for advice to Grandfather Lover. A liberal education might have been provided right in the old gentleman's parlor, for he had been a friend of such men as Byron, Dickens, Thackeray, Paganini and Thomas Moore, and the house was always filled with good talk and good company.

But Lover advised the widowed Mrs. Herbert to educate her son in Germany, where the schools were just as good and the costs were somewhat lower. Upon her remarriage, to Dr. Carl Schmidt, the family moved to Stuttgart and Victor entered the Humanistisches Gymnasium to prepare for the medical profession.

There are several versions of how he began his musical career. According to his own story given out at an interview in 1921, his mother bought him a flute, which he painted a gay yellow. But the paint smell was so strong and so ever-present that she finally begged him to take up some other instrument—the cello.

According to another version, it was not the flute but the piccolo, and when a schoolmate taunted him about it, he decided on something more suited to his own rather impressive size. At any rate, it seems fairly definite that on at least one occasion he did play the piccolo. At school, with an important festival coming up, he was offered a chance to substitute for an ailing piccolo player. Anxious to seize this opportunity (What boy would miss performing at a festival?), he mastered the instrument in two weeks and made his formal musical bow playing the piccolo part in the overture to Donizetti's *Daughter of the Regiment.*

Actually he had learned not only piccolo, but piano and

flute as well, before seriously taking up the cello at fifteen. This thorough grounding in musical instruments was to stand him in good stead for the rest of his life.

As for the rest of his education at the Gymnasium, not too much is known. Years later, in America, he told a reporter: "I had to study till one o'clock at night in order to keep up in my Latin and Greek, and the way we were taught made it stick. I can still quote my *Iliad*."

He seems to have been a good student, but financial difficulties in the family made it impossible for him to continue at the Gymnasium. He withdrew at sixteen and began studying the cello in Baden-Baden with Bernhardt Cossmann.

Among the distinguished musicians he met during his two years in the Cossmann household was Anton Rubinstein, who was Tchaikovsky's teacher. Rubinstein approved his progress with the cello. "You've got the build for it, my boy," he said. "Good strong fingers." There were other famous men of music, too: Saint-Saëns, Liszt, Brahms. Some critics have seen the influence of the two last named in some of Victor Herbert's gypsy and Hungarian music. Certainly he used folk tunes in his music, as did Brahms.

After two years with Cossmann, Herbert began to earn his living as a cellist with small orchestras. He was not yet nineteen. For four years he traveled through Germany, Switzerland, France and Italy, acquiring an intimate knowledge of instrumental music and a variety of languages. In later years, as conductor of the Pittsburgh Symphony, he could and did address the men of the orchestra in whatever language they spoke, switching from French to German to Italian to English as easily as switching from left to right.

It was during this four-year period of touring with

orchestras that Herbert first thought about composing his own music. At first it was largely improvising at the piano. But when he returned to Stuttgart as first cellist with the Royal Court Orchestra, he began studying composition in earnest with Max Seifritz.

He made amazing progress. In three months he had completed a Suite for Violoncello and Orchestra in five movements, and within a year he had written his first Concerto for Violoncello and Orchestra. The original manuscript of this work is now in the Library of Congress in Washington.

In Stuttgart Herbert was paid a fairly good salary, but like most young men, he often found himself "broke." He said later that he frequently couldn't afford to pay his laundress and so had to wash his own clothes and hang them outside his window to dry. But such minor inconveniences were nothing to a man as young and full of hope as Victor Herbert.

About this time he met Therese Foerster, prima donna of the Court Opera in Vienna. She was a beautiful young woman, gifted with a fine voice. The two young people fell in love and were engaged to be married.

At this point Frank Damrosch entered the picture, to alter the lives of both Herbert and his fiancée. Damrosch was an important American musician and critic. His brother, Walter, was Wagnerian director at the Metropolitan Opera in New York. When Frank Damrosch heard Therese Foerster sing, he immediately signed her up for the Met and offered Herbert a position as first cellist with the orchestra. The young people were married in Vienna that summer of 1886, and sailed immediately for New York.

In America Victor Herbert was to become the greatest figure in his chosen field.

Mrs. Herbert was well-liked by American audiences, but after that first season in New York, she never appeared in opera again. She had a young, ambitious, creative husband with a career of his own to think about, and she felt that her place was at home.

Victor had become immediately and enthusiastically American. He took out citizenship papers as soon as the law allowed. He had already known English, but he rapidly acquired the American idiom. His music, too, was American in boldness and authority. According to critic Cecil Smith, he assimilated American life and tastes "so thoroughly that he was generally considered an American composer from the beginning of his Broadway career."

But Broadway hadn't happened to Herbert yet. He continued playing in the Metropolitan Opera orchestra, and composing serious music: another cello concerto, a serenade for stringed instruments, an oratorio. He also appeared as soloist or guest conductor with other orchestras, and was identified with the Schmidt-Herbert string quartet, a popular ensemble of the time.

Through a friend, music critic James Hueneker, he was appointed to the faculty of the National Conservatory of Music. The famous Czech composer, Anton Dvořák, was the director of the Conservatory, and the two men became friends. Here, too, he met other great men of the musical world.

But while his attention was being devoted largely to serious music, he couldn't keep the lighter things out of his mind. In the year 1894, eight years after he had come to America, two things happened which were to shape his future career. One, he became bandmaster of the Twenty-Second Regiment of the New York National Guard; two, his first operetta appeared on Broadway.

This work, *Prince Ananias,* was composed for the Bostonians, the same light opera company which had made such a success with De Koven's *Robin Hood* four years earlier. As a matter of fact, it was the business manager of the Bostonians who introduced Herbert to Harry B. Smith, who had written the book for *Robin Hood*. With Smith, Herbert was to write his first hit show, *The Wizard of the Nile*.

It must be confessed that *Prince Ananias* was no *Robin Hood,* but at least it opened the way for Herbert. From that time until his death in 1924, he was seldom far away from the world of the theater. He and Smith collaborated on fourteen operettas altogether, including *The Serenade, The Fortune Teller,* and *Sweethearts*. With other librettists Herbert wrote twenty-eight other light operas, bringing his total in this field alone to over forty. With his songs, instrumental works, and two grand operas, Herbert was one of the most prolific of composers.

Many critics felt that when Herbert accepted the leadership of a regimental band he was turning his back on serious music, but this was not true. Many of his symphonic suites and other orchestral works were composed after this time, and at the same time that he was writing for the stage. The man was versatile.

He believed that there was no such thing as light music or heavy music. "To me there are only two kinds of music," he said, "good and bad."

Herbert is said to have told Walter Damrosch, "I am going to write comic operas until I make enough money to write what I want." But listening to Herbert's operetta tunes, it is difficult to see how he could have kept them from coming out, even if he had wanted to!

Herbert's first great success in the light opera field is largely forgotten today, sixty years after its opening. But one thing from *The Wizard of the Nile* remains, and that is the slang expression, "a wiz"—for someone exceptionally clever.

In 1897 came *The Serenade,* which has long been regarded as one of the finest examples of American light opera. The star was a newcomer, Alice Nielsen, whom Mrs. Herbert had discovered. She was awed by the opportunity, and more than a little frightened. Herbert personally taught her one of the songs. "If you forget the words," he told her, "just make up something. If you forget the second verse, repeat the first!"

Later Miss Nielsen recalled: "I never could have gotten through that first performance if it hadn't been for his enthusiasm. Power and energy—and a dash of Irish pigheadedness—that's what he had."

A similar reaction was voiced by another prima donna, the late Fritzi Scheff, for whom Herbert wrote *Babette* and *Mlle. Modiste*. "He had his Irish temper, and I had my Austrian one," she recalled. "When we clashed there was a little excitement."

Almost every year from 1894 on, there was a Herbert operetta. In some years there were several—three in 1899, for instance, and fourteen in the years between 1904 and 1909. At the same time he continued composing serious music, conducting, and performing with the cello.

With all this activity he kept up a happy and active family life. There were two children, Ella and Clifford. Herbert enjoyed playing with them, whether it was baseball at their summer home on Lake Placid or toy trains at their town house in New York.

Once he took them to an amusement park in New Jersey. Of course they rode the Ferris Wheel, and as luck would have it, they got stuck at the top. Far from being distressed, Herbert laughed so loud that he could be heard above the sound of the merry-go-round! The children, too, were part of Mr. and Mrs. Herbert's social life, which included some of the great names in music.

Ella, now Mrs. Robert Stevens Bartlett, recalls that many famous people came to dinner and to spend musical evenings. Her father would tell her, "Now, you don't have to talk, but just listen to these people talk." Afterward there would often be music by Fritz Kreisler, Caruso, Schumann-Heinck, or another of Herbert's gifted friends. Of course he never asked them to perform—they were professionals. But music just came naturally.

No one but a man of prodigious energy could have kept alive and healthy on the regime Herbert set for himself. After four years with the regimental band, he was conductor of the Pittsburgh Symphony Orchestra for six years. In 1904, he organized his own orchestra in New York. Almost until the day of his death he remained active in the concert field—one of the most demanding of all musical endeavors.

Once a friend told him he was working too hard. Herbert answered: "Nature really intended me to be a ship's stoker. I can stand it." And it was true. Over six feet tall and weighing more than two hundred pounds, he was tireless. He was particularly fond of walking at a brisk pace, and is said to have worn out more than one companion on these treks. Librettists who worked with him at Lake Placid were continually returning to the city exhausted from the business of working their minds as well as their bodies to the breaking point.

Fortunately, Herbert was also a warm, human individual. Between him and the men of his orchestra there was always a close camaraderie. He used to borrow small sums from them when he needed pocket money, and at the end of the season he'd simply ask: "Do I owe anybody anything?" Someone always spoke up.

On the other hand, he usually carried a few extra dollars in his pockets to lend to friends and chance acquaintances. He was considered a "soft touch," and no needy musician ever made an appeal to him which went unanswered. Once when he was rehearsing a show, one of the young men in the chorus was taken suddenly ill. Herbert found out later it was because the lad hadn't been eating regularly. He took the boy aside and gave him twenty dollars. "Go eat your head off," he told him.

There have been many stories told about Herbert's Gargantuan appetite. According to his daughter, Mrs. Bartlett, these tales are grossly exaggerated. He was a big man, and he enjoyed food and drink as much as any normal man of his size. But he needed a great deal of food to supply the energy he expended.

One famous story concerns *The Red Mill,* which was produced in 1906. For some reason it was one of those shows which went badly all through rehearsals. This, in spite of the fact that it contained some fine Herbert songs—"In Old New York," "Because You're You," and "Every Day Is Ladies' Day with Me." Later years and frequent revivals have proved the show's worth, and it was a hit on Broadway. But a few days before its opening the producers were ready to drop the whole idea, it looked so bad.

The final rehearsal took place on Saturday and lasted until four-thirty Sunday morning. Everyone was exhausted—except the tireless Victor Herbert. He took Henry Blossom, the stars of the show, and the director out for breakfast—with champagne! It revived them all, pepped them up, and gave them courage to go on. Result: the show was an enormous success.

Peggy Wood, of "I Remember Mama" fame, recalls that as a very young girl she played in the chorus of one of Victor Herbert's musical shows. From the orchestra pit, where he was conducting rehearsals, he would shout at the cast angrily, tear off his coat, run his hands through his hair in an effort to exact from them the very best that was in them. "But he was always friendly," she remembers. "I was surprised that he took any notice of me, but he did. He said he liked the name of Peggy because it was the name of a girl in one of his Grandfather Lover's songs."

According to Miss Wood, Herbert never *walked* anywhere—he always went at a dog-trot. That is Otto Harbach's memory of the great man, too. Herbert always did everything at top speed.

This facility came in handy more than once. As bandmaster with the Twenty-Second Regimental Band, he once composed a trumpet polka between the afternoon and evening performances at Washington Park, New Jersey. Again, during rehearsals for *The Fortune Teller,* he discovered that there was no time for Alice Nielsen, the star, to change her costume. Herbert stopped the rehearsal, sat down and wrote, on the spot, ten bars of new music for the tenor.

With the Pittsburgh Symphony, Herbert was ready to conduct an important concert with a guest soprano when he discovered that the orchestral score for her aria had not arrived. Only a short time remained before the performance. Herbert got to work at once and wrote the whole thing—some fourteen pages of instrumental parts—in time for the concert.

In the years that followed the first World War, Herbert, like most other composers of the older, gentler school, found their works less in demand than jazz and ragtime. Between 1917 and 1924, he spent more of his time on serious composition, and in the interests of Irish patriotism, than on operettas. He had written two grand operas, *Natoma* in 1911, and *Madeleine* in 1914. Parts of the score of *Natoma* are still heard today—particularly the "Dagger Dance."

In 1914, too, Herbert was instrumental in forming an organization which is today one of the most important groups of its kind. At that time his operetta *Sweethearts* was playing in New York. One night he dropped in at a restaurant just around the corner from the theater. The orchestra was playing all the hit tunes from this show!

Indignant, Herbert called his friends Gene Buck, John Philip Sousa, and others. They set up a plan whereby the composers and lyricists of musical compositions would be able to protect themselves from unlicensed performances of their works without payment or credit. The plan developed eventually into the American Society of Composers, Authors and Publishers (ASCAP), and has been of great benefit to both writers and the public.

Several years later, Herbert went with some of his colleagues in ASCAP to Washington, to ask that radio stations be forced to pay for the use of music which they broadcast. They were received by President Coolidge, who was most cordial and sympathetic. Herbert turned to a friend and whispered, "That's fine, but I'm still going to vote for Al Smith!"

The last operetta Herbert wrote was *The Dream Girl,* in 1924, the year of his death. Many critics consider *The Serenade* his finest, but *Naughty Marietta* is undoubtedly the most popular. The latter was made into a motion picture some years ago, with Jeanette MacDonald and Nelson Eddy. "Ah, Sweet Mystery of Life," the most memorable song from the score, was not in the original operetta at all, except as theme music (without words). It was the leading tenor, Orville Harrold, who suggested that words be put to the melody. The song sold so many copies that the publishing company of Witmark is said to have grown rich on it.

Herbert continued to be active until his death. On the morning of the day he died he had delivered a manuscript to his publisher and gone to the Lambs Club for lunch. There he told friends that he felt fine, "could eat a ton of nails." An hour later he was dead, the victim of a heart attack.

But his music, and his towering achievements in the world of musical comedy and operetta, have made him truly one of the immortals of the American scene.

HARRY B. SMITH

THIS is a story about a man nobody knows.

Ask anyone you like: "Who was Victor Herbert? Who is Irving Berlin?" Chances are you'll get the right answer: a song writer.

But ask that same person "Who was Harry B. Smith?" Unless he's a real old-timer in the theater, he won't know. Even in the early 1900's, when Smith was at the height of his career, only a handful of people could have told you who Harry B. Smith was.

Yet Smith was an important man. His part in the songs you sing today, such as "My Little Gypsy Sweetheart" and "They Didn't Believe Me," was almost as vital as the composer's part. For Smith wrote the words.

Basically, he cannot be called a writer of songs. Instead, he was a "librettist." In simple terms, that means a man who writes the book—the plot, the play, the spoken dialogue, and often some of the song lyrics as well—for a musical show.

Too often the librettist's star is eclipsed by the composer's. Certainly that was true of Smith, who worked with all the great men of musical comedy from Reginald De Koven to Irving Berlin. But although his name may not be as well known as Oscar Hammerstein's or Lorenz Hart's, his place in the history of the musical stage is unquestioned.

To tell a little of Harry B. Smith's story is to bow gently in the direction of all those other great "unknowns" who helped make musical comedy what it is today. Many of them were famous in their own right—and in their own day—but most of them have been forgotten except by theater critics and chroniclers.

But before we get into Smith's story—one that is as full of incident as the script for *Peck's Bad Boy*—let us try to find out just where he fits.

Most critics agree that *The Begum,* by Reginald De Koven, marks the start of light opera in America. Harry B. Smith wrote the book.

Robin Hood is one of the most memorable of these early comic operas. Harry B. Smith wrote the book.

The operettas of Victor Herbert represent a high spot in the history of the American musical stage. For several of these, Harry B. Smith wrote the book.

Irving Berlin's *Watch Your Step* was considered a turning point in musical comedy. Harry B. Smith wrote the book.

And so it goes.

You may have noticed that we have used four different terms for the same thing in the paragraphs above: light opera, comic opera, operetta, and musical comedy. Learned critics have written whole books on the likenesses and differences among these forms. But what we are talking about is a popular play with a sustained plot and recognizable characters, in which part of the action is advanced by musical numbers.

What did the librettist have to do with all this? In some cases all he had to do was to write the play. As in the case of Irving Berlin, the composer wrote his own lyrics. Occasionally the librettist would be called upon to write *part* of the lyrics, when the composer or the lyricist failed in inspiration. In other cases he might have to write *all* the lyrics. Sometimes a certain song or a certain situation would call for the talents of someone from the outside—to provide a funny sketch, write a few pages of dialogue, doctor a tune, or dream up some words.

When you know this, you realize that musical comedy is everybody's business. The producer, the director, the composer, the librettist, the stars, and sometimes even the star's relatives—all of these have a hand in the work.

That is why it is sometimes difficult to pin down credit for a single song or a single lyric in a hit musical.

To be successful in the musical comedy field, you must be a theatrical man-of-all-work. And Harry B. Smith was successful. He claimed to have written the words to six thousand songs, and to have had a hand in more than three hundred plays! He also wrote books and magazine articles in his "spare time."

He was born in Buffalo, New York, three days after Christmas in the year 1860. As a boy, he often heard his father and his uncles play an old-fashioned square piano, but music did not make too great an impression on him at first.

When his family moved to Chicago, Harry stayed with his grandparents in Buffalo for a while. Here he began to take an interest in books and reading. He used to go up into the attic and read old volumes that belonged to his grandfather

—*Great Expectations, Robinson Crusoe, Gulliver's Travels, Arabian Nights.*

Later he rejoined his parents in Chicago, where he entered school. His mother enjoyed going to matinees, and young Harry became acquainted with the theater and the opera. In Chicago he also saw his first "musical comedy," performed by the Lydia Thompson Burlesque Company, from England.

In those days—around 1870—there was no such thing as musical comedy as we know it today. Nor was the Lydia Thompson troupe anything like the "burlesque" chorus of today. Instead, the show was an evening's entertainment based on pretty girls, topical humor, lively tunes, and some dancing. But for a ten-year-old boy, it spelled magic.

It was around this time that the great fire destroyed most of Chicago, and the Smith family had to move. From his new home on the far North Side, Harry often had to ice-skate the two miles to school.

At school he was most interested in elocution, or public-speaking. It was already easy to see that he was headed toward a stage career for, at the tender age of twelve, he was hopelessly stage-struck. He recited so well that other classes came to hear him, and Harry Smith basked in their applause.

At the same time he was enjoying all the usual boyish sports: pigeon-hunting with his dad in the woods near their house, playing baseball with the Modocs (until a fast pitcher with speed and curves struck him out every time he came to bat), singing in the glee club, reading dime novels. He also undertook the publication of a newspaper, *The Weekly Seive* (with its title misspelled), which was an eight-page hand-lettered masterpiece that lasted just six weeks.

According to his memoirs, *First Nights and First Editions,*

Smith left high school after his first year, visited in Philadelphia and New York, and returned to Chicago "more stage-struck than ever." He took a job in a wholesale hardware house, while studying singing, dancing, and the banjo at night. One day his boss caught him practicing in the warehouse and fired him.

After a few more tries at routine jobs, he tried trouping with a traveling burlesque company and wound up broke in Philadelphia. In the meantime he had written one comic opera with a friend—but only as an amateur. His first published works were some verses in a Sunday School paper.

Now he drifted into theatrical and concert publicity and advertising. Among his clients was the Chicago Musical College, which was operated by Florenz Ziegfeld's father. Young Flo was not yet famous, of course.

He got five dollars for his first lyric, for a now forgotten song by George Schleiffurth. His first operetta was *Rosita; or Cupid and Cupidity,* which he wrote for actress Fay Templeton, on whom he had a crush.

But these were all just futile stabs at a career. After a few more tries, both at acting and writing, he got a job on the Chicago *Daily News* and worked his way up to music critic.

In the meantime he had met Reginald De Koven, another Chicagoan, and the two had started work on *The Begum.* Both had to work in their spare time, for De Koven had a full-time job at a wholesale dry goods house and Smith was still with the *News.*

Produced in 1887, *The Begum* was the first successful American operetta. De Koven and Smith were made. Although Smith continued to write and edit on the side, he never really left the musical stage thereafter.

His next operetta with De Koven was *Don Quixote,* in 1889. It was produced successfully by the Bostonians, but the main role was so demanding that the star is said to have declared: "Shelve the play or get a new comedian!"

It was, of course, *Robin Hood* for which De Koven is best remembered. When this play opened in Chicago in 1890, Smith was in the prompter's box, that hooded pit just in front of the footlights. He spent four hours in that spot, reading most of the dialogue to the actors, perspiring under the lights. The play was not too well received in Chicago, but when it returned after a tour, it played to packed houses.

In 1893, after several successful plays with De Koven, Smith gave up his newspaper job and moved to New York to devote all his time to the theater. While continuing his association with De Koven, Smith started working with Victor Herbert, whose star was rising.

Their first comic opera together was *The Wizard of the Nile.* It was Herbert's first big success as a composer of operetta. While little remains that is memorable about the book or the music, Smith can perhaps take credit for one thing. He contributed a new word to the English language with his catchline, "Am I a wiz?"

Altogether Smith collaborated with Herbert on fourteen operettas. For some of these, Harry's brother Robert wrote the song lyrics. Robert is credited, for instance, with the lyrics of the ever-popular "Sweethearts." Because of the number of hit shows they turned out year after year, Harry and Robert came to be known as "the inevitable Smith brothers."

Perhaps this is as good a time as any to consider some of the other librettists with whom Herbert worked. There was Henry Blossom, for instance. He wrote the books for *Mlle.*

Modiste, The Red Mill, and several other successful Herbert operettas. Born in St. Louis and brought up in the insurance business, he left the commercial world behind to become a writer. Although he worked with many others, including John Golden, who is no mean lyricist himself (he wrote "Poor Butterfly"), Blossom is chiefly remembered for his work with Herbert—and for the fact that he once danced a tango with such vigor that he broke his leg!

Then there was Rida Johnson Young, who did the libretto for Herbert's *Naughty Marietta.* If she had written nothing else, "Ah, Sweet Mystery of Life" would guarantee her immortality. She also wrote *Maytime* with Sigmund Romberg, and has the song "Mother Machree" to her credit as well. More than just a librettist, she was an author and an actress, too.

Glenn MacDonough, who wrote *Babes in Toyland* with Victor Herbert, as well as the lyrics for seventy-one other Broadway productions, began writing early. At the age of fourteen he wrote and produced a play, *The Prodigal Father.* His "Toyland" and "March of the Toys" are as familiar to most boys and girls as nursery rhymes.

These, then, were some of the principal writers who supplied the plays that made our musical comedies. Although all of them are now dead, the words they wrote are still alive.

But let us return to Harry B. Smith, who was in many ways typical of them all. His association with Victor Herbert continued for more than two decades. Many regard *The Fortune Teller* as their finest work, and it was in this show that "My Little Gypsy Sweetheart" was first heard.

When the show opened in New York, Smith made a curtain call speech to the effect that there was only one real first night, and that was in New York. It was one of those warm-hearted compliments that are delivered without thought of repercussions. But the repercussions came. The Philadelphia critics heard about the remark and grew angry. When *The Fortune Teller* came to Philadelphia, they were cool.

Nevertheless the good people of Philadelphia liked the play, and it was such a success that it was taken to England, where it ran for some time.

In 1887 Smith had married Lena Reed, and they had one son. At the very peak of her husband's career, however, Mrs. Smith died. Subsequently he remarried, this time to an actress, Irene Bentley.

He had been interested in books ever since boyhood, and after his popular successes began to bring him wealth and fame, he turned to book collecting as a serious hobby. An indication of the value of his collection may be had from just one figure. He once sold a "handful" of his rare books for $90,000!

His enthusiasm for rare books was shared by Jerome Kern, one of the composers with whom he worked. Kern finally sold *his* collection for over a million and a half dollars!

The best known song resulting from Kern and Smith's collaboration was "They Didn't Believe Me." It was first heard in *The Girl from Utah,* in 1914, and today it is still popular. The show itself was a popular success, and the song was Kern's first big hit, but the critics were not too kind.

None of them, however, was quite so acid as the one who reviewed Smith's *Liberty Belles,* which he wrote for Elsie Ferguson. Observing that Smith had written the show in three weeks, the critic remarked that he wondered what Smith could have been doing all that time!

Once when Smith and Kern were working together on another show, the composer was asked to supply a melody in a hurry. He dashed it off on the back of a discarded orchestra part and handed it to Smith, who then wrote the lyric in a dressing room. The song, "You're Here and I'm Here," was a popular favorite. But the producer's only comment was: "You boys make your money too easily."

Another composer with whom Smith worked was John Philip Sousa, the celebrated bandmaster and composer of "The Stars and Stripes Forever." Though Sousa is remembered chiefly for his marches, he did write a number of operettas. Perhaps the best known is *El Capitan*.

Sousa, though a fine musician, was a terrible pianist. Smith once heard Sousa play the finale of one of their operettas on the piano and was appalled at how bad it sounded. He worried for a while, then asked the bandmaster to play "The Stars and Stripes Forever" on the same piano. It sounded just as bad, so Smith decided that perhaps the operetta finale was all right, after all.

It was. The show was produced successfully.

Among the other composers of musical comedy for whom Smith wrote librettos were Sigmund Romberg, Franz Lehar, Oscar Strauss, and Ivan Caryll. He also collaborated with the famous American novelist, Sinclair Lewis, on a musical comedy based on his "Hobohemia" stories, but this was never produced.

His old friend from Chicago days, young Flo Ziegfeld, called on Smith to write his Follies shows of 1907 (the first), 1908, 1909, and 1910. In fact, the very name of these shows was Smith's idea. Years earlier he had called his newspaper column, out in Chicago, Follies of the Day. Ziegfeld simply changed "the Day" to a year. He felt that there was an especially good omen in the title; "Follies of 1907" had just thirteen letters!

In Smith's long and busy life, he knew most of the important people of the theater, and had the privilege of working with many of them. He never allowed his outside interest in books and writing to flag. Even when he was not busy writing a musical play (which was seldom), he wrote magazine articles and books.

He was one of the charter members of the American Society of Composers, Authors, and Publishers (ASCAP). In fact, it was the Victor Herbert song "Sweethearts," for which his brother Robert wrote the lyric, that was responsible for the birth of the organization. For when Victor Herbert heard his song being played in a cabaret without any royalty fee, he determined that some sort of protection was needed. His long campaign finally led to ASCAP.

Smith died in 1936, just after his seventy-fifth birthday.

His story indicates that all those anonymous toilers who helped to make musical comedy history were more important than they may at first appear. Times have changed; the theater has changed. Musical comedy has grown up, and the integrated work of Rodgers and Hammerstein is a far cry from the patchwork quilt of former days.

But as long as there are voices to sing the old songs—the melodies of Victor Herbert, the words of Otto Harbach and Henry Blossom and Harry B. Smith—we shall be grateful for them.

GEORGE M. COHAN

It's a stifling hot day in July. The yellow sun is beating down on hundreds of close-packed bodies, lined up along the curb of the street. You're packed in so tight you can hardly lift your hand to salute the flag as it is carried proudly by. The pavement burns through the soles of your shoes. It's typical Fourth of July weather, everywhere in America.

Then the band starts to play—and suddenly, in the midst of all that heat and all those steaming people, you feel a chill along your spine, and you shiver!

That's what martial music can do to you, and that's the kind of music George M. Cohan wrote best. More than thirty-five years ago his song, "Over There," was the inspiration of a nation at war. It sold more than a million and a half copies, and it is still today a popular number in the repertory of marching bands.

"You're a Grand Old Flag," which Cohan wrote eleven years earlier, has proved to be even more durable. Today no patriotic occasion is complete without that song. And his

"I'm a Yankee Doodle Dandy" is almost as well known.

One of the standard jokes of the period between two wars was that George M. Cohan had made more out of the American flag than Betsy Ross. The remark was not intended kindly, but the long survival of his patriotic songs seems to indicate that there is more to them than mere money. They are a very real part of American music.

Cohan succeeded in making the Fourth of July his very own day. He celebrated it as his birthday, though there is some question whether he was actually born on July 4.

Ward Morehouse, theatrical critic and Cohan's longtime friend, says it was July 3. But Cohan was so much the actor, had such an innate sense of the dramatic, that the Fourth suited him better.

At any rate, there is no question about the year, 1878, or about the place: Providence, Rhode Island. That city was to be as much "home town" as Cohan was ever to know, for his family was in show business and that meant traveling all the time.

But because he went to school there, and spent some of his summers at Rocky Point, he could grow sentimental about Providence—so sentimental that when one of the local newspapers wrote unfavorably about his musical, *Little Johnny Jones,* he was deeply hurt and vowed never to return! He did return, however, years later, and the townspeople gave him a parade and a hero's reception. Afterward Cohan staged a banquet for the musicians down at Rocky Point, because they'd been kind to him as a boy. He hadn't forgotten.

Yes, Cohan was sentimental, but his sentiment was so mixed up with his sense of the dramatic and his natural wit that it was not always easy to know what came from the heart and what from the love of the spotlight. In his own life story, for instance, he wrote that while it took most youngsters several years to get through school, it took him only six weeks. At the end of that time the principal sent for him and said, "You're through!"

True story or funny remark, the fact remains that Cohan had little formal schooling. His parents were on the road most of the time, and by the time he was eight, he had joined them.

The spectacle in which young Mr. Cohan had a part was a western melodrama entitled *Daniel Boone on the Trail.* His role consisted of riding a donkey in the parade, playing second fiddle in the orchestra, and selling songbooks in the lobby. This performance was repeated for some six months, in small towns all over America, and young George soon became a seasoned trouper.

At the age of nine he spoke his first lines in a play called *The Two Barneys,* and from then on his life's pattern was set. Although he swore from time to time to "quit the theater," he never really got away from it. Only the fact that his final illness incapacitated him for two years prevented him from dying "on stage."

Cohan didn't turn to song writing until he had already triumphed at almost every other phase of show business. With his parents and his sister, Josie, he trouped the country playing county fairs and vaudeville houses, traveling stock and road shows. Once he played his own mother's father. Once he put on a blonde wig and did a "sister act" with Josie. He was "Peck's Bad Boy"—the mischievous forerunner of Red Skelton's "Mean Little Kid." He was a black-faced minstrelman. He played, he sang, he danced, and finally the Four

Cohans—Mother and Father, Josie and George—landed on Broadway.

It wasn't Broadway, really. It was Keith's Union Square Theater, downtown. But it was New York, the goal of every vaudevillian, and George M. Cohan was determined that the Four Cohans should make good.

A small, wiry young man with an aggressive chin and a chip on his shoulder, he was furious when he learned that the Four Cohans were to open the show. The first act in a vaudeville revue was generally acrobats or jugglers, something that could just as well be missed by those who arrived late, something that would not be spoiled by those who were still finding their way to their seats.

But first act was better than none, and George determined to make the best of it. He was known as a "fresh kid," perhaps justifiably. But he had a really solid record of accomplishments and was not averse to talking about them. Older show business people, while big-hearted and sentimental, were also inclined to be skeptical. They didn't offer the Cohan kid much encouragement.

This merely toughened his resolution to put on the greatest performance of his career. When it came his turn to solo, he did a buck and wing and gave the audience everything he had. He had never put more physical energy into any routine. At the end, exhausted, he fell back and awaited the applause. Not a sound came from the audience. Dead silence.

Somehow George got off the stage; but afterward, in his parents' dressing room, he was so angry that he picked up a water pitcher and hurled it across the room. It was a characteristic burst of temper, and not the first that he had ever shown. Mother and Father Cohan finally succeeded in calming him down and persuaded him to finish out the week.

By Saturday night he had heard the exciting sound of palm beating against palm in isolated sections of the house—not much, but enough to make him feel that perhaps, after all, he could win this tough audience. That night, he knew he had them. He could feel it across the footlights, even before his act was done.

And then, right in the midst of his fanciest steps, a fight broke out in the audience and George M. Cohan might as well have been dancing in a steel vault. He lost the audience and had to retire in shame and disgrace.

Afterward a stagehand said sympathetically, "Don't feel too bad, kid. It's a frame-up by Keith and Albee." They were the managers of the theater.

"But why should they want to frame *me*?" George asked innocently.

"For taking money for that act," the stagehand answered.

Again, it's a good story, told by Cohan himself—but whether completely accurate or tailored for a laugh is hard to tell. In any event, the Four Cohans' first experience on Broadway was not an unqualified success.

Sister Josie, however, had made something of a personal hit. It was characteristic of George that he gloried in this triumph, even though it was not his own. Cocky he may have been; fresh, too, and over-confident; but his loyalty to his family and their "one-ness" as a group cannot be questioned.

Once when George was about fourteen and the family was playing in Buffalo, New York, young George decided he'd had enough. Perhaps there had been some upset, his temper had flared, or he was fed up with trouping "the sticks." In any case, he bought a railroad ticket to New York out of his own money and decided he'd go it alone in the big city.

He had just finished packing his bag and was ready to leave when his father put in an unscheduled appearance. The elder Cohan took in the situation at once. "Next time you want to run away," he said, "you come and tell me about it and we'll all run away together."

On another occasion, when George was only a few years older, his father stepped in again at a dramatic moment. This time romance was involved. Down at Rocky Point George had met a young woman named Julia Mackay, a female baritone. She had glamor, she had excitement, and George determined to elope with her.

The first step in their flight was to take the paddle-wheeler from Rocky Point to Providence. It was in the course of this moonlit journey that they were apprehended by a private detective whom George's father had hired. Julia went back to the "ten, twent, thirt" (10, 20, and 30-cent vaudeville circuit), and George to the bosom of his family.

It was as a family group that the Cohans made their first successful assault on New York. (Even after Josie's marriage, his parents' retirement, and George's own successful career as writer, producer, and manager, the family occasionally appeared together on the stage.)

Success first came to the Four Cohans just as George was about to give up trouping entirely. He'd been writing songs and sketches with some success; he'd even turned to "doctoring" other people's plays. He had just about decided that he'd give all his time to these efforts when the family got an offer to play Hyde and Behman's Adams Street Theater in Brooklyn.

In those days (around the turn of the century, when George was still in his teens) Hyde and Behman's occupied a position somewhat similar to the Roxy or the Paramount in New York today. In other words, it was a pinnacle in the world of entertainment at a time when radio and television were unknown and motion pictures were only a novelty.

To be sure, Brooklyn wasn't Broadway, and again the Four Cohans had the opening spot in the show. But George was determined not to repeat the fiasco of Keith's Union Square.

This time fortune smiled. The Four Cohans opened to tremendous bursts of applause. When it was over, George made a curtain speech: "Ladies and gentlemen, by mother thanks you, my father thanks you, my sister thanks you, and I thank you." In all the years that followed, George M. Cohan never changed that speech, and it stands today as a byword and reminder of the cocky little Irishman who conquered Broadway.

The Four Cohans grew in popularity until they were able to command the then startling figure of $1,000 a week. The fortunes of the family—and of George M. Cohan—were made.

His own career, however, outlasted the others. George M. Cohan was much more than just a song-and-dance man, although there are many around Broadway who still prefer to remember him that way.

Cohan's first published song was "Why Did Nellie Leave Her Home?" He had drifted into song-writing just as he had into singing and dancing—as a necessary part of being a trouper. Without formal musical training, he approached the business of composing the way an old prospector is said to have approached the business of speaking French. When someone asked him if he could speak French, he replied: "Don't know. Never tried."

Cohan saw no reason why he couldn't write a song, so he did. "Why Did Nellie Leave Her Home?" may have been no masterpiece, but it was his answer to a challenge.

Today it is difficult to understand what place such songs filled; but in the 1890's vaudeville was almost the only form of low-cost, popular entertainment, and songs like this, comic or sentimental, had a great vogue. Today they survive chiefly as curiosity pieces, if at all; and "Why Did Nellie Leave Her Home?" is one that has been conveniently forgotten by all except old-timers of show business.

As a matter of fact, the song didn't attract too much attention even at the time. He got more satisfaction out of one he wrote for May Irwin, a prominent vaudevillian, when he was still in his teens. He got more money out of one called "Venus, My Shining Love," which he sold for twenty-five dollars and which he stoutly maintained was the best song he ever wrote.

His first big song-hit was "I Guess I'll Have to Telegraph My Baby." This was a blues song delivered in blackface.

But if these songs had been all that George M. Cohan wrote, he would not be remembered today. He once said that he wrote songs only because they were easier and earned more money than sketches. Aside from his early studies of the violin, he knew little about music. But the music that was in him came out, to the service of the theater; and it has survived longer than any of the plays it served.

Cohan worked very fast. It seldom took him more than twenty-four hours to compose a song, both words and music. "Over There" was conceived one morning in 1917 at his home in Great Neck, Long Island. At breakfast he read the news of the United States' declaration of war on Germany. Before leaving for the office he started scribbling words to a persistent bugle call he heard in his mind. Within a half hour he had finished the chorus. He penciled the rest of the song on scrap paper while being driven into the city by his chauffeur. The melody was all he needed. He could pick out a tune on the piano; there were others to do the actual writing of notes.

This facility with words, this ability to produce songs and sketches on short order sometimes worked against him. It meant that he always put off writing until the last possible moment. In 1923, for instance, he actually wrote the last act of *Two Fellows and a Girl* on the way to the town where the show was to open the next night!

Writing was merely a detail—and not the most interesting one, at that—of putting on a show. Much more exciting to Cohan were the staging, the rehearsals, the actual treading of the boards.

When he met Sam Harris, for instance, who was to become his partner in the producing business, Cohan talked volubly about an idea for a new show which he said was to be called *Little Johnny Jones.* Harris liked it and agreed to help stage the show.

"All I had then was the title!" Cohan confessed later.

Little Johnny Jones, when it was eventually produced, proved to be a hit, and from it came at least two songs that are still heard today: "Give My Regards to Broadway" and "I'm a Yankee Doodle Dandy."

Cohan had been launched in the musical comedy business precipitously after several of his songs and sketches had attracted the attention of a producer named Gus Hill. According to Ward Morehouse, Hill sent for young Cohan and asked him if he thought he could write a real musical comedy—book, lyrics, music, and all.

It was a big assignment, but George didn't hesitate. "Sure," he said.

"Fine," answered Gus. "How much do you want for half a dozen?" Hill might have been buying bolts of cloth or cans of peas, but Cohan responded like an experienced merchandiser. From that day on, he always had something on the shelves!

His first musical comedy, *The Governor's Son,* was produced in 1901. Expanded from a one-act play, it was successful on the road, but not in New York. After the success of *Little Johnny Jones,* however, Cohan turned out musical comedies with regularity. The Four Cohans were no more, Josie having gone on her own.

In 1905 came *Forty-Five Minutes from Broadway,* which contained the song hits "Mary's a Grand Old Name" and "So Long, Mary." This play launched the career of one of America's most beloved comedians, Victor Moore. In those days, however, he was far from the befuddled little man who rose to popularity on the stage, in the movies, and on radio and television. Instead he was a brash, tough "city slicker" transplanted to the suburban village of New Rochelle, New York, which was pictured in the play as a "hick" town.

The citizens of New Rochelle boycotted the show, called an emergency session of the Chamber of Commerce, sent angry releases to the metropolitan newspapers protesting the blot on the fair name of their village—and *Forty-Five Minutes from Broadway* did a booming business.

In subsequent years there were other musical comedies and revues. *George Washington Jr.* (1906) gave birth to "You're a Grand Old Flag." Cohan told the story of this song. On a motor trip the year before he had met a Civil War veteran who had been a color bearer during Pickett's charge at Gettysburg. Referring to the flag, the old man had said, "She's a grand old rag"—and that's the way Cohan wrote it. But the critics objected, so the word "rag" was changed to "flag," and the song as we know it today was the hit of the show.

In addition to his musical shows, Cohan also dramatized the "Get-Rich-Quick Wallingford" stories and wrote *Seven Keys to Baldpate* as a play. This was his first non-musical hit.

He also went to Hollywood, but his experience with the movies was disillusioning. After ten weeks at $30,000 a week, he returned to New York and said, "If I had my choice between Hollywood and Atlanta, I'd take Leavenworth."

Years later, however, Hollywood immortalized him in a film called *Yankee Doodle Dandy,* starring James Cagney. Although the movie idealized Cohan and added more than a pinch of fiction, it was highly successful. Early in 1954 word came from Hollywood that another musical film based on Cohan's life would be made. The Cohan role was to be played by Mickey Rooney, an actor who, in many respects, resembles the old trouper.

Cohan's career spanned almost sixty years in the theater, yet he tried to get out after the first thirty. In 1914 he produced a revue called *Hello, Broadway,* in which Peggy Wood was one of the featured players. Miss Wood recalls his wit and charm, but also the fact that he often grew angry at rehearsals, and that the famous Cohan temperament was often on display. It was because he sincerely loved the theater that he grew upset with those who treated it lightly.

Once he told a group of chorus boys who weren't paying

attention to his directions, "You never think about the show when you leave the theater, but I think about it twenty-four hours a day."

Once he grew so angry with an actor that he told the manager: "We'll never have this man in a show again—unless we need him!"

After *Hello, Broadway,* Cohan announced his retirement from the stage. His first, early marriage had ended in divorce, and he was now happily remarried and the father of two fine children. He wanted more time at home. But not even family ties could keep Cohan away from the stage. His "retirement" lasted exactly ten months. Then he was back, never to leave again till finally illness forced him out.

Not all of this time was spent performing, however. In fact, for many years he was primarily a producer and writer, until 1935, when the Theater Guild persuaded him to take the serious role of the father in Eugene O'Neill's *Ah, Wilderness!*

His performance in this part proved what the critics had known for years; that George M. Cohan was by all odds the most accomplished actor on the American stage. Later he accepted the role of Franklin Delano Roosevelt in *I'd Rather Be Right,* a musical spoof of American politics. Cohan didn't like the smart songs which Rodgers and Hart had written for this show, and on opening night in Boston he actually substituted his own lyrics. George S. Kaufman, coauthor of the play, had to ask him not to do it again!

On the whole, however, Cohan was generous to other show people. When Irving Berlin paid him a tribute, Cohan replied, "Now, there is a fellow who can really write a song."

When Billy Bryant, operator of a show boat, asked him for the rights to one of the successful Cohan musicals, Cohan recalled their early days together in vaudeville. He had written a sketch for the Bryants which had flopped. To make up for it, Cohan now turned over to Bryant the rights, free of all royalties for life, to one of his best musical comedies.

Many have criticized Cohan for his flag-waving, for his stubborn attitude as a manager against the actors in the Equity strike of 1919, for his cockiness, for his hot temper. But no one can deny that his songs are made of durable, lasting stuff.

You have only to hear them to agree.

Rudolf Friml

What makes a song last? Why do some tunes remain in memory long after the time when they were written?

If you can come up with an accurate answer to these questions, your fortune is made. You can retire and spend the rest of your life fishing and living off your royalties.

But the answer isn't easy. Men have spent whole lifetimes of effort, broken their hearts, and wasted their energies trying to find the formula of song success. They find it difficult to understand why the public will cling to a song that was popular in grandmother's day and reject one that is as new and fresh as tomorrow.

Again and again the phenomenon has been demonstrated by the men about whom this book is written. And looming large among them is a long-haired Czech immigrant named Rudolf Friml.

His first big hit was written in 1912. He reached the height of his popularity in the 1920's. Yet today his songs are still sung and hummed and whistled.

You can hear them any day on the radio or television. "The Donkey Serenade," "Sympathy," and "Giannina Mia" are all over forty years old. "Rose Marie" and "Indian Love Call" are over twenty-five. So are "Song of the Vagabonds" and "Only a Rose." How many of today's songs will last that long?

Yet Friml himself would probably be unable to explain *why* these songs have endured. All of them were written for the musical comedy stage, and therefore they met the strict requirements of story and theater. Perhaps that gave them added mettle.

Whatever the secret, music seemed to come from Friml effortlessly. One of his collaborators, Otto Harbach, recalls that he "poured melodies out of his sleeves." He composed by sitting at the piano and improvising, letting his fingers wander almost aimlessly. In later years he has traveled the world, played his tunes into a recording device, and sent the recordings home to his secretary, who then transcribes the notes onto paper and does any necessary arranging and instrumentation.

By the 1950's, however, Friml's musical output had fallen off to some degree. Like many another successful composer, he answered the call of Hollywood and found life there so much to his liking that he remained. If he has rested on his laurels, the rest is well deserved. For a period of more than twenty years, from 1912 to 1934, Friml composed at least one operetta each year, and often had as many as three in a year on Broadway!

They ranged from such semi-serious works as *The Vagabond King* to the frivolities of the Ziegfeld Follies. And if all of his songs have not endured to this day, enough of them have to ensure his place in the musical hall of fame.

The Bohemian composer did not start out to write for the

stage. At the outset he probably never dreamed that such names as Ed Wynn, Mae West, and Jeannette MacDonald would be featured in connection with his music. Instead he probably dreamed of opera houses and concert halls, where classical musicians of serious mien would perform his works.

Certainly his education led in that direction. He entered the Prague (Czechoslovakia) Conservatory of Music when he was fourteen. He studied piano with Josef Jiránek, and composition with the great Bohemian composer, Anton Dvořák, emerging as a piano virtuoso of great talent.

Today his graceful piano études are almost as popular, if not as well known, as his operetta tunes. They are standard items in the repertoire of most young piano students, and many of them have been scored for string orchestras, to become the kind of anonymous, tuneful music that is heard late at night on bedtime radio shows.

But young Friml had loftier ambitions at the start. By the time he was seventeen he was accompanist for the famous violinist Jan Kubelik. The two gave concerts all over Europe, and Rudolf soon built a reputation for himself—a reputation that was to bring him to America as a concert pianist.

He made his American debut at Carnegie Hall in 1904, playing his own "Concerto in B Major" with Walter Damrosch and the New York Symphony. He had accepted the engagement at the last moment, and there had not been time for him to score the piano part. Thus, at each rehearsal he played it differently, a fact that led to much confusion on the part of the other musicians.

Nevertheless, the young composer's American bow was a pronounced success. *The Independent,* a leading periodical of the day, reported on it as follows:

"Most interesting of the month's newcomers among virtuosi was Rudolf Friml, a young Bohemian pianist, who made his bow as a composer also by playing his own concerto with Walter Damrosch's orchestra. This piece was rather long, but there are some beautiful things in it and it was worth a hearing. Mr. Friml is undoubtedly a young man of exceptional talents."

Accompanying this paragraph was a photograph of the twenty-year-old Friml. His face was almost girlishly pretty, with large dark eyes and a sensitive mouth. He wore his dark, wavy hair long—some said in an attempt to look like Franz Liszt, though the effect was rather more like Chopin. All in all, Friml was, in 1904, the very model of a serious young musician.

He might have remained dedicated to classical music if it had not been for a curious chain of circumstances. Otto Harbach tells it this way:

In 1910 or thereabouts, the reigning queen of the New York musical comedy stage was Emma Trentini. She had scored an enormous success in Victor Herbert's *Naughty Marietta,* and Arthur Hammerstein (uncle of Oscar Hammerstein II) was anxious to cash in on this popularity with a new show. Even before *Naughty Marietta* closed, Otto Harbach had contracted to write another Trentini musical with Victor Herbert. This was to be *The Firefly*.

But at the closing performance of *Naughty Marietta,* the temperamental Italian star refused to sing a single encore. This so infuriated Herbert that he refused to write another note for her.

Both Hammerstein and Harbach hoped that Trentini might make some gesture of peace, or that Victor Herbert would weaken in his resolve. But as time went on and nothing happened, it became apparent that a new collaborator would have to be found. The book was already written. A score was needed. Rudolf Friml, the musician from Prague, had friends in the theater. They mentioned his name, and the rest is musical history.

Here the composer's great talent and facility were put to the test. He came through beautifully, and *The Firefly* was a hit. In the original score, one of the most memorable songs, "Sympathy," did not appear at all. (This seems to be a common theatrical accident; De Koven's great "Oh, Promise Me" was a last minute addition, too.) Instead, the melody was only incidental music played by the orchestra between scenes. A week before the show opened in New York, it became clear that another song was needed. Harbach obliged by adding words to the haunting tune, and "Sympathy" was one of the hits of the show. It is still a hit today.

The Firefly, like other Friml operettas, is still performed frequently. It is especially popular in summer outdoor theaters like the St. Louis Municipal Opera and the Paper Mill Playhouse in New Jersey. A few years ago it was made into an immensely popular movie starring Jeannette MacDonald and Alan Jones. And here again we run into an amusing story that illustrates the persistence of popular music.

While the movie was enjoying its greatest success, one of the songs, "The Donkey Serenade," appeared time and again on the popular radio program, "Your Hit Parade." Youngsters who went around humming and whistling the "new" hit did not realize that it was a hit of some twenty-five years earlier. Herbert Stothart had dressed up some of Friml's "incidental" music from the original score, and with new words it became "The Donkey Serenade."

As recently as 1951, "The Donkey Serenade" was winning a whole new generation of fans, thanks to recent popular recordings.

The Firefly, then, set Rudolf Friml on the road to musical comedy fame and fortune. He remained an aloof young man, and those who knew him best described him as charming but erratic—more a man of the concert hall than of the theater. But the theater was to be his home for the next two decades. *Katinka,* which he composed a few years after *The Firefly,* ran for 220 performances in an age when ragtime and jazz were already beginning to make operettas seem tame. According to Cecil Smith's book, *Musical Comedy in America,* one reason for its success was the presence of a great vaudeville performer, A. Robbins, in the third act. His performance consisted of "pulling an endless variety of incredible objects, large and small, out of his baggy trousers" and was one of "the funniest moments of the evening."

Other Friml operettas, however, seem to have survived without vaudeville. Both *Rose Marie* (1924) and *The Vagabond King* (1925) passed the 500-performances mark. Both starred Dennis King, who is today perhaps better known as a dramatic actor than as a musical comedy star. Both have been frequently revived, both off and on Broadway. And both were made into spectacularly successful motion pictures.

One of the songs from *Katinka* was a number called "Rackety Coo," which old-timers of the theater still recall affectionately. It is seldom heard today, but was revived in 1952 on television, with the same sort of production it received originally. What made it notable both on the stage and on

TV was not Friml's catchy melody nor Otto Harbach's engaging words but the fact that the singer is accompanied by a flock of trained pigeons which fly in from the wings of the stage on cue.

Two numbers from *Katinka,* however, *are* memorable in their own right. One is " 'Tis the End, So Farewell," and the other is "Allah's Holiday." The latter is a favorite number with high school orchestras.

Otto Harbach recalls that Friml could improvise in any style. He could take a simple tune and play it as a Russian kazitsky, a Hungarian polka, a French minuet, or an English country dance. He could render it in the style of Mozart, Wagner, Chopin, or Liszt. In more recent times such performers as Alec Templeton and Victor Borge have demonstrated this same gift. Friml has also the gift of *original* melody.

After *Katinka,* it was some years before Friml had another really big hit, though he contributed steadily to Broadway. He continued to write more serious music too, and the whole body of his compositions during these years forms a respectable library of music. One show presented about this time is worth mentioning, however. It was *Sometime,* with the great comedian, Ed Wynn.

Mr. Wynn, whose crazy costumes and antics have been beloved by generations of theater-goers, and by television-viewers as well, recalls that he "altered the book of this show and collaborated in one song with Rudolf." If one can believe reviews of the period, Ed Wynn is being unduly modest. He did, in fact, make the play.

According to Cecil Smith, *Sometime* broke through the conventions of operetta—"not because Friml intended it to, but because a man by the name of Ed Wynn would not let it alone." Lost in the cast of this same show, which was produced in 1918, was a young actress named Mae West. But it was Wynn who drew critical acclaim.

A truly successful composer for the musical comedy stage learns early in his career that his music is the tool of the playwright and the players. It must never outshine them, and yet it must support them. It cannot be dull, but it dare not be brilliant—at least not more brilliant than everything else about the show. While the play is on, the music is only incidental. When the play is over, the music may or may not last.

For that reason there is no harsh criticism intended in these observations about Friml's music. It is, in fact, a tribute to his genius that so many of his musical comedy songs have survived and are still being sung today.

Friml's real forte was in writing sentimental, graceful melodies that seemed to belong to another age. In the period after the first World War, when jazz began to flourish, his kind of music remained popular with a limited audience, but it had to bow to the new mode. Friml tried his best, but was none too graceful.

In 1919, for instance, he was called upon to write the score for a show called *Tumble Inn.* This included music for shimmy dancing and a low-comedy song. Friml protested that this was not his kind of work. But he had not yet made a great enough reputation that he could afford to turn down the show. He did the score, and it is significant that nothing about *Tumble Inn* has survived today.

There were also innumerable Ziegfeld Follies, but Mr. Ziegfeld was a showman of such good taste and judgment that Friml was able to write music more to his liking. Besides, Ziegfeld was a valuable friend to have, for he produced not only the annual Follies show but also other important musicals.

It was with *Rose Marie* in 1924 that Friml really came into his own. Here he proved that he could write music for the theater and still sacrifice nothing in quality or substance. Dennis King played the leading male role of the Northwest Mounted Policeman, while Mary Ellis was Rose Marie. In movie versions of the operetta, the leading roles were played first by Nelson Eddy and Jeannette MacDonald, and later by Howard Keel and Ann Blyth.

According to J. Walker McSpadden in his book *Operas and Musical Comedies, Rose Marie* found favor with a large audience "by reason of its contrasts—the simplicity of the wilds, with the sophistication of society." Scenes ranged from a pass in the Canadian Rockies to a ballroom in the Château Frontenac. And the music—all of it tuneful, memorable, and refreshing—ranged from the rousing "Song of the Mounties" to the haunting "Indian Love Call."

After this triumph, Friml was on top of the musical comedy world. But he did not rest. Instead he went to work writing *The Vagabond King,* an ambitious musical play based on Justin McCarthy's *If I Were King*. This operetta, produced in 1925, was to clinch Friml's reputation. The play itself was more substantial than anything else he had adapted; the music was—and is—better than any of his previous efforts.

In addition to the "Song of the Vagabonds" and "Only a Rose," there are at least half a dozen other songs which remained popular. These include "Love for Sale," "The Huguette Waltz," and "Some Day."

Friml's last big hit was *The Three Musketeers* in 1928. It was given a sumptuous production by Flo Ziegfeld. Dennis

King played the role of D'Artagnan. The music was tuneful. The story, based on Dumas's great novel, was exceptional. Yet at least one critic was unhappy with the show. The acid-tongued Alexander Woollcott wrote that he "did greatly enjoy the first few years of Act I."

After *The Three Musketeers* Friml continued to write for the stage until 1934, when he was swallowed up by Hollywood. The Bohemian boy who had picked out his first tunes at the age of four had come a long way. By ten he had written a boat song. By fourteen he had fallen in love and was writing love songs. From then on a steady stream of music had come from his pen.

Nor did he stop writing in Hollywood. Instead he provided the music for a few films, had time for the piano studies he had neglected, and above all, time for travel. Although he maintains a home in Hollywood, friends report that he is almost never there. Instead he is sailing the seven seas in his own yacht, recording music to be sent back to his faithful secretary and enjoying life.

In 1952 he startled the public by getting married, at the age of seventy-three. His bride was thirty-nine-year-old Kay Ling, a Chinese girl who had been his secretary.

But friends who know him well were not startled. "He's the most charming guy in the world," they say, "but unpredictable."

OTTO HARBACH

IF you have listened to the juke boxes or the radio disc jockeys at all, you've heard one or more of the songs of Otto Harbach. They're not new songs; they're "old favorites." The fact that they are still popular in this modern day is just another proof of their greatness.

Harbach writes words, not music. But his words have become so inseparable from the melodies they grace that it's impossible to think of one without the other.

Merely to run over the list of titles is enough to set you singing: "Smoke Gets in Your Eyes," "Cuddle Up a Little Closer," "The Desert Song," "Indian Love Call," "Who," "The Touch of Your Hand." These are just a few of Harbach's works. He has written more than a thousand songs, and some of them are performed somewhere in the world every day.

In addition, Harbach has worked with most of the finest composers of musical comedy: Rudolf Friml, Sigmund Romberg, Jerome Kern, Vincent Youmans, and George Gershwin, to name a few. His lifetime of work has spanned from the earliest days of musical comedy in America to the present. As fifth president of the American Society of Composers, Authors, and Publishers (ASCAP), he won recognition of his place in the history of American music. He is, indeed, the dean of librettists.

Too often it is the composer who gets all the credit, while the man who supplies the words that make the music into song is forgotten. This is natural enough, particularly when the composer is as celebrated as Victor Herbert or George Gershwin. But those in the know—the people of the theater, the singers, actors, producers—realize that the libretto can make or break a musical show.

When words and music fail to meet and match, the result is awkward and ugly. A true work of art results only when words and music blend perfectly. It is a tribute to Otto Harbach's artistry that his words have become an immortal part of our musical heritage.

A tall, vigorous man with a shock of gray hair, Harbach in his eighties was more alert than many a man half his age. It is easy to see that he came from pioneer stock.

Thoroughly American, he was born in Salt Lake City, Utah, in 1873. His parents were good, hard-working Danish people. As a child he wanted three things: a piano, a saddle horse, and a trip to New York. But the family was too poor to provide any of them.

With a little imagination young Otto made the horse-hair sofa in the parlor his make-believe piano. Like thousands of other youngsters, the only horse he ever owned was a broomstick. And for a long time it looked as though he would never get closer to New York than Galesburg, Illinois.

It was at Galesburg that young Harbach went to college,

after finishing his studies at the Collegiate Institute in Salt Lake City, where he was a classmate of the great actress, Maude Adams. Ambitious for more education, Harbach rode east as far as Chicago with a carload of sheep. He finally reached Knox College in Galesburg—a town which is also celebrated as the birthplace of another American poet and singer, Carl Sandburg.

Harbach worked his way through Knox, and was graduated with a Bachelor of Arts degree. He then went to Walla Walla, Washington, where he had been engaged as a teacher of English at Whitman College. After six years there, he saw his dream of New York about to come true.

In those days it was still customary for colleges to grant their instructors "sabbatical leaves." These occurred every seven years—hence the term "sabbatical"—and Harbach determined to take his leave in New York and study at Columbia University. New York was an exciting city at the turn of the century. Theaters were buzzing with excitement and activity, music was in the air, great figures could be seen dining at famous restaurants. To the boy from Utah it was all fascinating.

He says that once he saw New York, he knew he could never live anywhere else in the world. So he decided to stay. He worked on a New York newspaper for a year—this was in 1901—then switched to advertising as a copy writer. The firm for which he worked, the George Batten agency, later became Batten, Barton, Durstine & Osborn, or BBD&O, one of the biggest companies in the advertising business.

Harbach stayed six years with Batten. While there he wrote plays at night, fulfilling a youthful ambition that had started when he used to do odd jobs for a quarter and promptly spent his quarters for balcony seats in the nearest theater. His plays were spectacularly unsuccessful at first. He says that he once spent eight years trying to develop a play with a Western theme, and it was never produced.

But Harbach believes that no honest effort is ever wasted. At any rate, in 1909, a musical show he wrote with the composer Karl Hoschna proved to be a hit on Broadway. It was *The Three Twins,* and all that survives of it today is the beguiling song, "Cuddle Up a Little Closer."

Hoschna was a Bohemian composer who had come to America and won a place in the Victor Herbert orchestra. Turning to operetta, he enjoyed quite a vogue on Broadway. Perhaps his most successful effort was *Madame Sherry,* which appeared in 1910. Again Harbach wrote the book. The success of this play ensured his future career as a musical comedy librettist, and set the long path of melody he was to travel.

The hit song from *Madame Sherry,* "Every Little Movement Has a Meaning of Its Own," is still popular today, despite its rather obscure title. Harbach explains that in the play, "Every Little Movement" was sung by a young woman who was teaching a class of debutantes aesthetic dancing. He chuckles over the puzzled and somewhat labored interpretations that radio and television announcers sometimes give that song-title!

Madame Sherry cost $35,000 to produce—a mere pittance compared with today's hundreds of thousands of dollars. There were only three simple sets and a cast of eight boys and four girls. At one time there were six separate companies playing *Madame Sherry* in various parts of the world, a record rivaled in later years by such hits as *Oklahoma!* and *South Pacific.*

After Hoschna's death in 1911, Harbach contracted with Victor Herbert for *The Firefly*. But when the temperamental star, Emma Trentini, and the adamant composer could not settle their differences, another composer had to be called in. The composer was Rudolf Friml, and thus a second profitable and lasting collaboration began for Harbach.

He never did a show with Victor Herbert. The two men had worked together on one play, but Herbert's death occurred before the work was completed. Harbach recalls that Herbert was a perfect dynamo. He did everything at top speed. Once Harbach spent three weeks with the great man at Lake Placid. "When I left I was a sick man," he recalls. "I couldn't stand the pace." For Herbert not only worked hard, he played hard, too, indulging in long, brisk walks, violent exercise, and quick plunges into the lake.

Harbach's collaboration with Rudolf Friml continued for more than a dozen years and resulted in such lasting favorites as *Katinka* and *Rose Marie*. The two men worked easily together, particularly since Friml turned out melodies at such a rapid pace.

Friml was not the easiest composer Harbach worked with. Jerome Kern, for instance, had a better story sense. He always understood the needs of the drama, something which was occasionally difficult for musicians. Harbach's association with Kern was to prove one of the smoothest blendings of talents in the history of the theater—but more of that later.

Harbach's last big success with Friml was *The Wild Rose,* in 1926. Meanwhile he had written shows with other composers as well, notably Louis Hirsch, Vincent Youmans, and Jerome Kern. Of the Hirsch operettas, little remains that is heard today, with the exception of one song, "Love Nest," written for *Mary* in 1921. This, in spite of the fact that Hirsch was one of the most prolific composers ever to write for Broadway.

In the 1920's, that hectic decade which has been described as the jazz age, Harbach entered upon his most productive period. He had married Eloise Smith in 1918, when he was 45, and started a family. Perhaps the two sons who blessed this marriage were partially responsible for the ambition which led Harbach, during the twenties, to turn out one musical comedy hit after another. In the year 1926, he had five shows in production at one time!

Great names of the theater graced the casts of his shows: Marilyn Miller, whose life story was made into a successful movie, *Look for the Silver Lining;* Clifton Webb, of *Mr. Belvedere* fame; Bob Hope; Eddie Cantor (Harbach wrote *Kid Boots* for him at Ziegfeld's request); and many others remembered by an older generation.

In 1923, Harbach wrote his first show with the brilliant young composer, Vincent Youmans. It was called *Wildflower,* and the score was fresh, rich, and colorful. Although the songs from this show are not often heard today, they established Youmans as a musical comedy composer. He had made a name for himself as an assistant to Victor Herbert and had already done one Broadway musical. *Wildflower* was another big step forward.

In 1924 the two men collaborated on another show, *No, No, Nanette!* which was a hit of substantial proportions. It had a long, successful run in New York, and was produced in London, in every important European capital, in South America and New Zealand. Road companies continued to play it throughout the United States long after the initial thrill had passed off Broadway.

There is an interesting sidelight on *No, No, Nanette!* The production of a big musical show then, as now, required the talents of many different persons. With an opening date looming in the too near future, it was sometimes necessary to call for outside help. A sketch, a song, a set of lyrics might be contributed by someone other than the librettist. That's what happened with *No, No, Nanette!*

The man who was called in to help was Irving Caesar, who was later to originate the "Sing a Song of Safety" jingles which are widely used in public schools throughout the United States. And the two songs for which he wrote the lyrics were the biggest hits of the show—and still hits today. They are "Tea for Two" and "I Want to Be Happy."

Youmans and Harbach did one more show together, *Oh, Please!* in 1926. Their collaboration was cut short by Youmans' illness and his increasing interest in more serious music.

Harbach recalls that Youmans was one of the most talented young writers in the theater, but rather aloof and temperamental. He was always very ambitious, not just as a composer of musical shows, but as director, producer, and everything. A short, slender man with a deep voice, he always whistled his melodies before writing them down. His untimely death at the age of forty-eight was a great loss to the theater.

In this same period belongs Harbach's first show with Jerome Kern, *Sunny*. Written expressly for the great dancing star, Marilyn Miller, it was produced successfully in 1925 in New York and later in London. One of the greatest songs to result from this show—or any other show—is the never-to-be-forgotten "Who?"

This song, with its simple melody, logical structure, and driving rhythm, lends itself to all sorts of interpretations. On one hand you may hear a deep-down blues singer asking who stole her heart away; on the other hand it may be shouted joyfully over the strains of the brass section. It's a smooth dance tune; but it is also a dramatic monologue. Any way you look at it, it's a great song—and its versatility is what makes it great.

With Kern, Harbach also wrote *The Cat and the Fiddle* (1931) and *Roberta* (1933). The first of these two musical plays is chiefly memorable for two songs: "She Didn't Say Yes," and "The Night Was Made for Love." It was the first musical show without a chorus, an innovation which was to reach its zenith in Rodgers and Hammerstein's *South Pacific*.

Roberta was perhaps the finest work of the Harbach-Kern team. The score contained all these fine songs: "Yesterday," "Smoke Gets in Your Eyes," "The Touch of Your Hand," "I Won't Dance," "Lovely to Look At," and others. It is also a memorable show for having introduced to a wide American audience a young comedian named Robert Hope.

Roberta was made into a successful motion picture with Irene Dunne, Fred Astaire, and Ginger Rogers. It has been revived at various summer operetta theaters, notably the St. Louis Municipal Opera. But even without revivals, the rich music of Jerome Kern and the perfectly blended words of Otto Harbach would continue to be sung.

Kern's innate sense of the dramatic made him an ideal composer to work with; and in turn, Harbach's assured knowledge of musical requirements was an added advantage to the team. As a boy, Harbach had studied violin. When writing lyrics, he often used the instrument as a means of giving them musical shape and substance. In fact, it is impossible to conceive of any successful librettist who is not also, instinctively, a musician.

Proof of the skill and adaptability which took Harbach to the top of his profession is his collaboration with so many different composers, each with a different style. It would be difficult to think of two composers more opposite in style than Rudolf Friml and George Gershwin; yet Harbach wrote with both.

True, the one Gershwin show he wrote was not typical of that breezy, modern composer. It was *Song of the Flame,* composed in 1925, and a far cry from Gershwin's later successes, *Of Thee I Sing* and *Porgy and Bess.* It was out-and-out operetta of the old-fashioned school, and Gershwin shared musical honors with Herbert Stothart, a composer better known for motion picture than for stage music.

The most memorable song from this production, and one which is occasionally heard today, was "Song of the Flame." A movie production in 1930 helped to popularize the music.

Harbach's story would not be complete without mention of *The Desert Song.* This fabulously successful operetta was composed by Sigmund Romberg, one of the most prolific of all musical comedy composers. After its successful opening in New York in 1926, it enjoyed a long run in London. It is still frequently performed, and was notably revived on Broadway in 1946. It was also given two separate motion picture productions, the second one in 1952, starring Gordon MacRae.

All of these productions, plus the memories of everyone who has ever heard the songs, have served to keep the music from *The Desert Song* very much alive. And Harbach's libretto, which he wrote in collaboration with Oscar Hammerstein II, contributed greatly to the operetta's popularity.

With all of these successes, Otto Harbach remained a modest, unassuming man. Until his term as president of ASCAP ran out in 1953, he reported at his desk in a New York skyscraper every day, commuting from his home in nearby Mamaroneck, New York. Though no longer writing, he kept very much in touch with the musical theater. The walls of his office were covered with the photographs of the great stars of stage and screen with whom he has worked, and with the less familiar faces of writers and producers whose names loom great in the world of music and the theater.

The boy from Salt Lake City finally got to New York—and New York will never forget him.

Sigmund Romberg

Almost three years after Sigmund Romberg's death in 1951, New York newspaper columnists were writing about *The Girl in Pink Tights,* a new musical comedy on Broadway —"with music by Sigmund Romberg." Not "the *late* Sigmund Romberg." Just his name.

Probably a great percentage of the people who read such items thought Romberg was still alive. They had every reason to think so, for every year since about 1912 there had been a steady stream of melody from his pen.

Even those who were still shocked and saddened by Romberg's passing from the scene had little reason to be surprised by the opening of a new work. It was known that he had been working on a musical comedy at the time of his death. A year without a Romberg tune would be like a year of drought.

To emphasize his immortality, one Romberg tune was a popular favorite as late as 1953. It was a song he'd written twenty-five years earlier, "Lover, Come Back to Me"—in a jazzed-up, be-bop version, to be sure, but still Romberg and still a hit.

Sigmund Romberg is considered by many to be the most versatile and the most prolific of all American musical-comedy composers, even exceeding Rudolf Friml and Victor Herbert. On the score of versatility, Exhibit A would show such widely varying tunes as "Pretty Baby" and "Deep in My Heart." On the score of volume, Exhibit B would fill several pages.

For Romberg wrote over two thousand songs, and had a hand in over seventy-five musical productions for the stage, radio, and motion pictures! He was also widely known as a performing artist in concert and radio, and he once took on the formidable task of composing original operettas for a weekly radio show!

He kept so busy during his lifetime that it would take several lifetimes to hear and appreciate all his music. For a penniless lad from Hungary who came to America as a young man and worked for seven dollars a week, he made quite a substantial reputation.

Sigmund Romberg was born in 1887, in a Hungarian city with an unpronounceable name—Nagykanizsa. His father was a businessman, but an amateur musician as well. He saw to it that Sigmund was exposed to the violin at about the age of six. At eight, he was studying piano as well.

He was sent to school at Osijek (now in Yugoslavia), and in his first year there was admitted to the school orchestra. This was a signal honor, since most students were not allowed even to try out until they'd finished four years of schooling. But Romberg's fiddling was so amazing that the orchestra director took him in immediately.

Transferring to a smaller school where there was no orchestra, Romberg organized one himself within a few weeks. He was now in his teens, and completely at ease in front of a band or orchestra. He took up the study of theory, harmony, and counterpoint, acquiring a solid background in these arts.

At sixteen, while a student at still a third school, he composed the "Red Cross March" and dedicated it to the Grand Duchess Clotilde, sister of the Emperor of Austria-Hungary. When the great lady gracefully acknowledged the compliment, Romberg and the whole town of Szeged went crazy. It was a rare distinction for the town and for the school.

The school orchestra numbered only eighteen hardy young musicians. As a reward, Romberg was allowed to draw upon the town's military band for additional men. He now had forty, the biggest group he had ever conducted. But according to Elliott Arnold, whose *Deep in My Heart* tells much of the Romberg story, he was not at all abashed. Instead he ordered the burly Army men to shave off their beards and moustaches, so they wouldn't look so different from the students!

Although Romberg was now firmly imbedded in the musical world, his father intended him to be an engineer. With this in mind, he was sent to Vienna to enter the Politechnische Hochschule.

At this point Romberg found himself in a dilemma similar to that of many young men today. He was faced with compulsory military service, and his career as an engineer seemed remote and far away. Besides, he had become acquainted in Vienna with the glamorous world of the theater.

Among other notables, he had met Franz Lehar, composer of *The Merry Widow* and other light operas. Lehar introduced him to Heuberger, one of the finest teachers of composition, and later gave him a letter of introduction to J. J. Shubert, the American theatrical producer. Romberg was to use that letter when he came to America—but that was later.

Meanwhile he told his parents that he wanted to leave school and enter the world of music. His father was shocked, but finally consented to let the boy make his own decision—as soon as he had completed his year of military service.

It wasn't a bad year. Romberg was stationed in Vienna, in those days still the center of the musical world. His fellow-soldiers were good companions, and together they frolicked through the city, enjoying the usual pranks and escapades of young men everywhere.

But he was a good soldier. After his compulsory year, he put in eight months of active service. Then he returned to his parents' home, and finally persuaded them that a trip to America was just what he needed.

He landed in New York in 1909 with a little money, the address of a cousin in the Bronx, and the Lehar letter. He filed the letter away for future reference and went out to find a job.

He got one, packing pencils in a pencil factory for seven dollars a week. The other workers brought their lunches from home, but Romberg wanted to get out and see more of this friendly, democratic city, symbol of a whole new world. One day he decided to have lunch at a Second Avenue café (he had to borrow a quarter to do it). While he was enjoying his Hungarian goulash, he struck up an acquaintance with another customer.

The second man was also Hungarian, and a musician. He offered Romberg a job playing piano in his orchestra at a

Hungarian restaurant downtown, at fifteen dollars a week, and "all the goulash he could eat." Romberg jumped at the chance, and thus launched one of the most remarkable careers in show business.

From fifteen dollars a week and goulash, he went to twenty-five dollars a week and chicken in a Harlem restaurant. By the time he was making forty-five dollars, he had applied for citizenship in the United States and was determined to make this country his permanent home.

Soon he was able to shift from pianist to conductor, at Bustanoby's, the most famous Hungarian restaurant in New York, and probably the world. It was a dignified, dressy sort of place, but the young man with the classical education couldn't keep his feet still. He wanted to introduce dinner dancing to create new business.

At first André Bustanoby was horrified at the thought. Then he said, "Go ahead and try. You'll see. No one will dance."

He was right. Although the restaurant advertised dinner-dancing, the customers were just too timid to try this new-fangled idea. On the sly, Romberg hired two couples, ambitious youngsters in show business, to pose as customers and start the ball rolling. His stunt worked. The idea caught on, business boomed, and Bustanoby's raised Romberg's pay to $150 a week.

Along about this time he started composing. According to one story, a popular composer of the time dropped in one night and heckled Romberg: "Why don't you play some good music—some of mine?"

"Rommy" answered scornfully, "I could write better stuff myself—overnight."

A Broadway publisher overheard this conversation and said: "You do and I'll publish it."

The next day Romberg turned up with his first popular composition—a one-step called "Some Smoke."

This number, along with a turkey-trot called "Leg of Mutton" and a waltz, "Le Poème," which he also wrote in this period, grew popular at Bustanoby's and helped to make Romberg's reputation. He was ready for the plum which was soon to fall in his lap.

It came about through J. J. Shubert, the same man to whom "Rommy" had a letter of introduction from Franz Lehar. Shubert, with his brothers Sam and Lee, controlled the most powerful theatrical leasing and producing enterprise in the city at the time. To be singled out for Shubert favor was the pinnacle of many a young showman's ambition.

The prolific Louis Hirsch had been so singled out and had served as staff composer for various revues and other musicals in which the Shuberts were interested. But he had a falling-out with them in 1912, and they were looking for a new composer. Romberg got the job.

His first assignment was to write the music for a Winter Garden Revue, *The Whirl of the World*. Revues are no longer very popular on the American stage. Perhaps the public today gets its fill of songs, sketches, and production numbers—totally unrelated to each other—on radio and television. But in 1913, when Romberg wrote his first score, revues were as inevitable on Broadway as chorus girls.

For the next four years, as a matter of fact, Romberg was to devote most of his talents to writing scores for Shubert revues. There were two musical plays during this time: *The Midnight Girl* (1913), and *The Girl from Brazil* (1916). But neither of these was a great success. There was also an operetta imported from Vienna for which Romberg wrote a hit song, *"Auf Wiedersehen,"* which is still heard today.

But for the most part Romberg simply manufactured music for *Passing Shows*. The Shuberts kept promising him a "real musical play," but first there was always one more chore to be done: a song for Marilyn Miller, an Al Jolson show, another importation.

During this period, Romberg grew intimately acquainted with the problems of singers and theater musicians. He was influential in the development of unions to protect these people, and to raise their pay scale. The same sort of businesslike concern for members of his profession was to lead to his active participation in ASCAP and the Song Writers' Protective Association, in later years.

The Shubert brothers, true to the tradition of Broadway producers, knew the value of pretty girls. But Romberg thought that musical ability was more important. He used to hire singers who were good, whether they had "looks" or not. Then he would have to place them in the back of the stage, carefully concealed behind a façade of gorgeous showgirls, to keep the Shuberts from spotting them.

Romberg is credited with giving Vivienne Segal her start, in *The Blue Paradise*. Miss Segal, gifted with both good looks *and* a voice, was then a young music student at Philadelphia's Curtis Institute. Frightened and nervous about her stage debut, she was unable to give her best, and Romberg's tearful song *"Auf Wiedersehen"* came out wooden and ineffectual.

On opening night the stage manager had an idea. Just before Miss Segal was to go on, he took her aside and scolded her unmercifully. He was so rough with her that she cried.

On cue, she rushed onto the stage with tears rolling down her cheeks and delivered *"Auf Wiedersehen"* with all the heartfelt emotion that anyone could ask. The song was an immediate hit—and so was Miss Segal. She was a star from then on.

In 1914, Romberg had been called upon to make a grave decision. As a reserve officer in the Imperial Austro-Hungarian Army, he was called to the colors of his native land when World War I broke out. To obey the summons would have meant forfeiting his chance to become an American citizen. Feelings of patriotism to the land of his birth were mixed with new-found loyalty to America. He decided to stay in this country.

In 1918, after the United States entered the war, he was inducted into the American Army and served in military intelligence till the war's end.

A year earlier, however, he had written his first really important musical show, *Maytime*. The star was Peggy Wood, then a young stage actress and years later a star on television in "I Remember Mama." Lyrics were by Rida Johnson Young, the same librettist who had written *Naughty Marietta* with Victor Herbert a few years earlier.

This show produced one really great song, "Sweetheart," which Miss Wood sang as a duet with Charles Purcell. Sometimes known as "Will You Remember," this song has become a familiar light classic that might have been written in another age than the frantic, war-torn year of 1917.

After the war, Romberg felt secure enough in his reputation to leave the Shuberts. With a friend he had formed his own music-publishing company, and the future looked bright. But the venture was doomed to failure. The firm collapsed after two years of struggle and Romberg, $50,000 in debt, had to go back to the Shuberts.

They offered him *Blossom Time,* the story of the great German composer Franz Schubert. What was involved was the adaptation of Schubert's music to the "popular" vein. At first Romberg bucked at the assignment. He had no taste for cheapening great classical music. But broke and in debt, he had to accept.

Blossom Time turned out to be one of the most fabulously successful productions of all time. It enriched everyone who had anything to do with it, and particularly the Shubert firm, which is still sending out road companies to play it in remote parts of Australia! It has been performed professionally more than five thousand times, and it is still going strong.

"You Are My Song of Love" is probably familiar to more Americans than is Schubert's Unfinished Symphony, upon which it is based. Other Schubert melodies received similar treatment in the play. If *Blossom Time* did nothing else, it aroused public interest in the great music of the past.

It was probably because of this adaptation that a recurring story began to be told. Less successful composers, frustrated critics, and jealous performers started saying that Romberg "borrowed" his tunes from others. It is a charge that has been leveled at almost every great man. Shakespeare had his Bacon; Victor Herbert was accused of plagiarism; De Koven was said to have taken credit for a music copyist's work.

Victor Herbert took his fight to court—and won. Others have simply laughed off the charges as vicious smears. Romberg used to laugh at the story, too.

Peggy Wood remembers that the walls of his study were lined with operatic and symphonic scores. When she commented on them, "Rommy" chuckled and said, "I know where to go if I need them."

He once told a friend that it would be perfectly safe to bet any composer $10,000 he couldn't write an original tune. Some "expert" will always be able to track down a similar one that has been written before.

However, Romberg's next big success disproved this. For *The Student Prince,* produced in 1924, was a completely original score. Romberg had started work on it immediately after *Blossom Time,* but a number of pressures interfered. First there was the breakup of his first marriage. Then his father in the old country became seriously ill, and Romberg was called upon to raise money for an operation. With legal and medical expenses piling up, and some of his debts still unpaid, he needed ready cash. To raise it he took on no less than six assignments simultaneously, while still trying to work with Dorothy Donnelly, his *Blossom Time* librettist, on *The Student Prince.*

One night he collapsed on stage and was forced to take a long rest. During this time Miss Donnelly introduced him to Lillian Harris, and the two fell in love. After Romberg's recovery and the success of *The Student Prince,* they were married in 1925.

But *The Student Prince* was not an immediate hit. It opened in Atlantic City in 1924 as *Old Heidelberg,* but its reception was mild. Since Romberg had given it the better part of two years' loving care, it was a great disappointment to him. But the Shuberts decided to bring the show in to New York, anyway. Only one change was made: the title. As *The Student Prince* it was an instantaneous hit in New York. There were nine separate companies playing it at one time in the United

States alone, and like *Blossom Time,* it has been a road company success over the years. Its performance record is nearly as good as that of *Blossom Time.*

Scarcely anyone in America can have escaped hearing "Deep in My Heart" or "Serenade," two of the most beautiful and enduring melodies from the operetta. "Golden Days" and the lusty "Drinking Song" are almost as well known.

Following the success of *The Student Prince,* Romberg's place in the world of music and the theater was established. He returned to Europe, to Osijek, to see his parents. While there he hired an auditorium and a sixty-piece orchestra to perform a concert of his works, for just two listeners—his mother and father!

Upon his return to America, he parted company with the Shubert brothers and set to work immediately on a new operetta to be called *My Lady Fair.* His collaborators were two of the best-known librettists in the business, Otto Harbach and Oscar Hammerstein II. *My Lady Fair* promised to be a spectacular success.

And it was, under the title *The Desert Song.* First produced in 1927, it had a long run on Broadway and in road company tours. It was revived on Broadway in 1946 and was made into a motion picture twice, the last time in 1952, starring Gordon Macrae. Romberg had given the rights to *The Desert Song* as a present to his wife, Lillian.

It had a bad start, however. On the opening night a main fuse blew out in the theater. One of the ceiling beams broke and the scenery fell down. A donkey ridden by one of the characters was upset by the music and began to bray noisily. But the charm of the story and of the tunes Romberg had written won out, and the audience loved the operetta.

The "theme song" of the play, "The Desert Song"—sometimes called "Blue Heaven and You and I"—was another one of those last-minute additions. It was written in two days, just before the opening. Today it is by far the best known of all the music in the play.

Oscar Hammerstein II has recalled "Rommy's" methods of working. He was a hard taskmaster, according to Hammerstein. As soon as one song was completed, he'd ask: "What else have you got?"

Their usual way of working was for "Rommy" to study the book, then sit down at piano and begin to improvise while Hammerstein listened. After a while, the librettist would take the music and disappear for a week or two. When he returned, he would read the words as Romberg played the music. "Rommy's" only comment usually was, "It fits." Then they'd turn it over to the singers.

At rehearsals Romberg was aggressive and demanding. He used to pound a heavy cane on the floor when dissatisfied. But basically he was a gentle kind of man, who loved to entertain, who liked people, good food, and good drink.

This has been testified to by another colorful theatrical figure, Mike Todd, who produced Romberg's *Up in Central Park*. "He was a great guy with the groceries," Todd recalls. "He always ate at the best restaurants." And on the subject of Romberg's temperament, Todd laughs. "That was strictly phony," he insists. "'Rommy' used to get sore, but right in the midst of it he'd break out in a laugh."

The Desert Song and *The New Moon,* also written with Hammerstein, probably represent the pinnacle of Romberg's career. It is true that after 1928 he wrote more operettas and songs—including such a deathless one as "When I Grow Too

Old to Dream" for a Hollywood movie—but he is best remembered for these two works, *The Student Prince* and *Blossom Time*.

He collaborated with George Gershwin on one show, *Rosalie,* which Florenz Ziegfeld had commissioned for Marilyn Miller. But he was working with Hammerstein at the same time on *The New Moon,* while Gershwin was writing still another show. As a result, *Rosalie* suffered.

Nor was *The New Moon* a success in its tryout period. After that Romberg actually had to write a second version of the show, and it was for this version that the great song, "Lover, Come Back to Me," was composed. According to Elliott Arnold, he wrote it in a half hour before dinner one night!

Romberg also had a brief association with composer Richard Rodgers, for *The Poor Little Ritz Girl* in 1920. It was Rodgers' first teaming with Hart, and Romberg had his own lyricist. Actually the two composers did not work together, but each supplied part of the music.

In 1929 Romberg went to Hollywood to write original musicals with Oscar Hammerstein II. From then on, much of his time was to be spent in motion picture work, radio, and concerts. He did write a few more operettas worth mentioning: *May Wine* in 1935, one of the first musical shows to use a murder-mystery as the basic plot; *The Girl of the Golden West* in 1937; *Sunny River* in 1941 and *Up in Central Park* in 1945, his last Broadway success before his death.

In 1941 he formed his own orchestra, which he conducted in immensely popular coast-to-coast tours. He also entertained soldiers and sailors during World War II. At one such concert in Atlanta, the train was late, the auditorium too small, and the musicians had to play on the lawn outside the hospital without dinner. When they were through, there was terrific applause from the patients, many of them in wheel chairs. And the commanding officer said, "That's the best medicine my patients have had in months!"

Romberg remained active and writing until the very end. He died in New York in 1951, while at work on *The Girl in Pink Tights.* After his death, Hollywood set to work on a movie about his life. Its title was, appropriately, *Deep in My Heart.*

JEROME KERN

A SMALL, white-haired man with bright, blue eyes and an alert, birdlike expression stood, somewhat baffled, in the Hollywood spotlight in 1944. National magazines wrote articles about him; he was photographed at work and at play; glamorous actresses and movie stars paid him tribute.

Yet he was neither a producer, a director, nor a playwright; he was no actor, nor even an actor's agent. He did not write a gossip column, nor conduct a radio show.

He was only a composer, and his name was Jerome Kern.

The reason for the celebration was that Kern had been in show business forty years. For once, Hollywood had seen fit to honor a great composer while he was still alive to enjoy it.

Yet Jerome Kern belonged more to Broadway than to Hollywood. His greatest movie successes had been adaptations of plays which had first been presented on the stage. And when the sound and the fury were over, Kern returned to Broadway and was engaged in plans for a new musical when he died.

His career had begun in Tin Pan Alley in 1904. He was hired at seven dollars a week to play popular songs in department stores. From that modest start he rose to the status of millionaire composer, even before the golden hands of Hollywood reached out for him.

Sheet music sales of his songs almost invariably reached the two-million-copy figure. Before he died he had composed songs for more than fifty musical shows and movies. His music was the inspiration for many another composer, including even the redoubtable George Gershwin. And at least one of his musical plays—*Show Boat*—is an immortal part of the American theater.

Altogether, Kern fully deserved the praise that Hollywood heaped upon him a year before his death. Yet he remained modest, quiet, and somewhat detached from all the hubbub. He looked like a scholar, and in many ways he acted like one, too.

Efforts to glamorize him had him wearing orange trousers and a green shirt to rehearsals; had him composing while the radio played full blast. Yet he chose as a hobby the collecting of rare books—a pastime that only a thoughtful, scholarly man could enjoy.

In 1928 he sold his collection of books for $1,800,000—obviously he was no mean businessman, either. But the first thing he did afterward was to buy an especially rare volume that he had always wanted but hadn't thought he could afford.

So Kern was a mixture of practical businessman and sentimentalist. A story from his early years illustrates the point.

His father was a merchandiser with interests in furniture and other commodities. In 1902, when Jerome was only seventeen years old, the elder Kern took him into the business, then located in Newark, New Jersey. Jerry's first assignment was to cross the river into New York and buy two pianos from a dealer.

The youngster was so enthralled with his first business deal that he ended up taking two hundred pianos instead of just two! His father was irate when he learned what Jerry had done—especially since there was no way out.

But the story has a happy ending. The elder Kern arranged to warehouse the pianos and to sell them on the installment plan—at a neat profit. Nevertheless he was so shaken by young Jerry's lack of business judgment that he agreed to let the boy go to Germany to study music.

Music had played an important role in his early life. Born in New York in 1885, he had enjoyed the companionship of two brothers. The three boys, with their mother, were soon playing eight-hand piano concerts in the family parlor.

After the family moved to Newark, Jerry played the organ at school, and also composed music for high school shows. He entered the New York College of Music, already confident that he was going to become a composer. But his father had other ideas.

Then came the episode of the pianos, and Jerry won his point. He was shipped off to Heidelberg. When he returned in 1904, with the degree of Master of Music, he went into Tin Pan Alley—the toughest training ground possible for anyone with ambitions to write "hit" songs.

During this time he was also accompanist for Marie Dressler, a famous vaudeville performer and later "Tugboat Annie" of movie fame. Through contacts with various performers and music publishers he began to acquire the background which was to lead to a life-long career in the musical theater.

His first published song was "How'd You Like to Spoon with Me?" But he was still several years away from "hit" classification. That song appeared in 1905. For the next few years Kern worked and lived in London, where he was connected with producer Charles Frohman's office.

In England Kern met many persons of prominence in the theatrical world, and in the world of literature and music. Later he was to team up with Guy Bolton, British librettist, and with P. G. Wodehouse, another Englishman famed for his humorous writings, to write some of the brightest musical shows ever seen in America. But this was not till years later.

While in England Kern also met another person who was to play an important part in his life. She was Eva Leale, daughter of an innkeeper at Walton-on-Thames. The two young people fell in love and were married in 1911, after Kern had returned to America.

Mrs. Kern said later that during the year when Jerome was gone and she remained in England, he wrote her just two friendly letters. The third was a formal proposal of marriage.

When Kern returned to America, he was still far from affluent. His experiences in England had provided him with good friends and excellent background, but he was still a "struggling, young composer." He maintained a connection with the T. B. Harms Company, music publishers, but his main job consisted of writing the opening musical numbers for shows imported from Europe.

Often Kern's contributions were brighter than anything in the original score, but they did not bring him fame and fortune. They simply provided him and his new bride with a steady income in the field to which he had decided to dedicate himself.

Even in these numbers, however, he was demonstrating the originality and thorough musicianship which were to characterize his later works. By 1912, when his first original musical comedy, *The Red Petticoat,* appeared, Kern had a small but devoted following, but the larger public was still unaware of his talents.

In 1914 Kern scored his first big hit with a musical comedy called *The Girl from Utah.* This, too, was a British import, and most of the music was by Paul Rubens and Sydney Jones. But one Kern song from this production has remained popular to this day: "They Didn't Believe Me," first sung by Julia Sanderson.

It doesn't always happen that first success means turning the corner and living happily ever after, but in Jerome Kern's case it did. From 1914 on, the composer never passed a Broadway season without either being represented by or planning a big musical show, until he went to Hollywood at the peak of his career in 1934.

In 1915 he did four shows, the first of which was *90 in the Shade,* with Guy Bolton. It was important largely because it brought these two first-rate talents together. But a show they did later that year was a hit of much more substantial proportions. This was *Very Good Eddie,* which ran for a year on Broadway and another year on the road.

Very Good Eddie deserves mention here principally because it was one of the first musical comedies to have coherent plot and dialogue—something which had heretofore been the concern chiefly of nonmusical plays. An "intimate" musical comedy designed for a small theater and audience, it was the first of its kind in America.

Now Kern settled down to the steady production of one or two shows every season. He had certain ideas which were ahead of their time. He insisted, for instance, that the music and lyrics be an integral part of the show, not just casual numbers interpolated into the action. He also felt that the old-fashioned "girlie-girlie" chorus was unnecessary. He wasn't able to "sell" all these ideas, but he made some progress.

He worked with other composers—notably Victor Herbert, on *Miss 1917* and *Sally*—and with other librettists, such as Otto Harbach and Oscar Hammerstein II. A 1918 success was *Leave it to Jane,* based on George Ade's play, *The College Widow*—the Hoosier humorist's one excursion into musical comedy. Kern also produced such memorable songs as "Who?", "A Wild, Wild Rose," "Look for the Silver Lining," and dozens of others.

In *Sally,* which Florenz Ziegfeld produced for the brilliant dancing star, Marilyn Miller, Kern included a song called "Whippoorwill." The critics pounced upon this number and complained that it was not an authentic reproduction of the birdcall.

"Of course it isn't," Kern agreed. "George M. Cohan already used the authentic call in 'Over There'!"

In addition to his musical comedy chores, Kern had become a partner in the T. B. Harms Company and breathed new life into the business through the soaring sales of his own songs, as well as those of other composers. Years later a rival music publisher, Edward B. Marks, recalled in his memoirs, *They All Sang,* that Kern had once worked for him, making out bills and invoices in a jobbing plant. Later, when Kern had some money to invest, he had offered his services to Marks in exchange for a junior partnership, but Marks let him go!

Thus did Harms profit from Marks' mistake.

In addition to such stars as Marilyn Miller, Kern's shows had featured other musical comedy "greats"—Leon Errol, he of the rubber legs; Clifton Webb, later famous as "Mr. Belvedere"; Al Jolson; Vivienne Segal; Elsie Janis, perhaps the most famous entertainer of World War I; Irene Bordoni; Ernest Truex, whom television fans will recall as the lovable grandfather of "Jamie"; and many others.

Still Kern hadn't created a real masterpiece, in terms of a completely integrated musical play. That was to come in 1927, with *Show Boat.*

Kern electrified the entire theatrical and musical world when he announced his plans in 1926. He intended to make a musical play out of Edna Ferber's best-selling novel about a Mississippi riverboat gambler and his young bride, the daughter of a showboat family. While the book had been enormously popular and critically acclaimed, most people felt that there were too much sadness and violence, too many stark problems, too brutally realistic characterizations for a successful Broadway musical.

Miss Ferber herself told Kern: "I always thought you were sane. How can you make an opera out of *Show Boat?"*

Kern, in turn, shocked her by saying: "I got a copy of your book but couldn't read it." When she asked why not, he explained, "I had to keep hurrying to the piano to work out the tunes that kept popping into my mind."

Later he said that the music wrote itself—and what music it is! "Only Make Believe," "Ol' Man River," "Can't Help

Lovin' that Man," "You Are Love," and "Why Do I Love You?" among others.

Perhaps "Ol' Man River" is the greatest of them all. As Edna Ferber recalls in her autobiography, *A Peculiar Treasure:* "I must break down and confess to being one of those whose eyes grow dreamy and whose mouth is wreathed in wistful smiles whenever the orchestra—any orchestra—plays 'Ol' Man River' . . . I just happen to think that when Jerome Kern wrote the *Show Boat* score he achieved the most beautiful and important light-opera music that has ever been written in America. And I consider Oscar Hammerstein's lyric to 'Ol' Man River' to be powerful, native, tragic, and true . . .

"As the writing of the musical play proceeded . . . I heard bits and pieces of the score . . . Jerome Kern appeared at my apartment late one afternoon with a strange look of quiet exultation in his eyes. He sat down at the piano. He doesn't play the piano particularly well and his singing voice, though true, is negligible. He played and sang 'Ol' Man River.' The music mounted, mounted, and I give you my word my hair stood on end, the tears came to my eyes, I breathed like a heroine in a melodrama. This was great music. This was music that would outlast Jerome Kern's day and mine. I never have heard it since without that emotional surge."

Nearly everyone has that same reaction to "Ol' Man River" —and to *Show Boat* as a whole. It has been successfully revived four times in New York, has been made into a movie three times. Even the critics, those monitors whose job it is to detect weaknesses and imperfections, agreed that *Show Boat* was a masterpiece. More than that, it was a turning point in American musical comedy.

Cecil Smith, in his book, *Musical Comedy in America,* says of *Show Boat:* "No other American piece of its vintage left so large a permanent musical legacy, and certainly no other surpassed it in quality."

It is interesting to note that one of the songs in *Show Boat* was provided with lyrics by P. G. Wodehouse, with whom Kern had collaborated in earlier shows. This was "Just My Bill," sung by the fragile and expressive Helen Morgan, who played the role of Julie. Wodehouse, with Kern and Guy Bolton, had formed a triumvirate which did much during the World War I era to revivify the musical stage.

In the years that followed *Show Boat,* Kern continued to contribute to the musical stage. And if his later productions were not masterpieces, it was partly because *Show Boat* had hit such a high mark. Chief among these later works were *The Cat and the Fiddle,* the first musical comedy without chorus girls; *Music in the Air,* with two great songs: "I've Told Every Little Star," and "The Song Is You"; and *Roberta,* Kern's last production before Hollywood.

Roberta was in many ways a remarkable show. To begin with, it boasted one of Kern's finest scores—music with strong emotional appeal, deft charm, and powerful imagination, including such songs as "Smoke Gets in Your Eyes," "The Touch of Your Hand," "Lovely to Look At," and "I Won't Dance." One of the most memorable numbers, "Yesterday," was sung by the aged aunt of the story just before she died peacefully in her chair.

In addition, *Roberta* featured an on-stage fashion show that Broadwayites are still talking about. And finally, it gave Bob Hope his start on a Hollywood career when the stage run was over. As a movie it also added considerably to the stature of Irene Dunne, Ginger Rogers, and Fred Astaire.

Soon after *Roberta,* Kern left for Hollywood, where he was to contribute many another fine musical score. Among his stage successes which were made into movies were *The Cat and the Fiddle, Music in the Air, Sweet Adeline,* and of course *Roberta* and *Show Boat.* He also composed the music for a Lily Pons movie, *I Dream Too Much,* and for some of the films made by Deanna Durbin and by Ginger Rogers and Fred Astaire.

He and Mrs. Kern and their daughter, Betty, lived in Beverly Hills, where he could hear the birds sing—an inspiration he sometimes needed. However, Kern was stubborn on the subject of "inspiration." He once told an aspiring song writer, "If you wait around for inspiration to light on your shoulder and gently poke the cobwebs from your brain, you had better change your profession." Instead he advised sitting down at the piano and improvising, not to complete a song at one sitting, but simply to get an idea, a striking combination of notes, or a few bars for a finished song.

Mrs. Kern told a reporter that he had an invariable way of deciding whether what he'd done was good. He'd play the melody on the piano while she hummed it. If she liked it, he'd throw it away! He usually worked in his study with a pipe in his mouth and a jar of candy at his right hand.

When writing for the stage he used to work at a rehearsal piano, and when he'd gotten what he wanted, he would summon everybody—stagehands, electricians, stars, anybody who was handy—to the piano. Then, with a bright, expectant look on his face, he would say, "I've got something for you," and play the new tune.

Kern made one more excursion to Broadway during his

ten-year stay in Hollywood. This was for a musical called *Very Warm for May,* in 1939. But the public did not like it and it is largely forgotten today.

In 1945, after his daughter had married, he and Mrs. Kern returned to New York where he was to start work on a new musical about Annie Oakley. The star was to be the dynamic Ethel Merman, and the producers, Rodgers and Hammerstein. While planning the production, Kern was seized suddenly with a heart attack and died.

Annie Get Your Gun was subsequently written by Irving Berlin—and a fine job it was. But sentimentalists can't help wondering what Kern would have done with this same basic story. It would have been interesting to make a comparison.

He always classed Berlin as one of his favorite composers, along with Wagner, Liszt, and Tchaikovsky. Legend ran that there were two busts on Kern's piano: one of Wagner and one of Liszt. When a Kern hit tune was born, the Wagner bust would smile!

IRVING BERLIN

To write songs that people sing is a difficult art. To do it successfully, even with years of musical education and training, is no mean accomplishment. But to do it without being able even to read music is almost a miracle.

That's what makes Irving Berlin something of a miracle man.

He had no musical education—little education of any sort. He can play the piano in only one key: F sharp. He cannot read a note of music. His own tunes have to be transcribed by a secretary. Yet he has written over a thousand songs, most of them hits, and many of them just as popular today as they were when first written.

If you doubt it, think of "The Easter Parade," which was written for a Broadway show in the 1930's; and "White Christmas," which first appeared in one of Bing Crosby's movies. Both of these Berlin tunes—and a dozen others—are as durable as diamonds.

Berlin himself somewhat pooh-poohs his song-writing

gifts. He admits to more than a thousand songs, but says actually they are only seven or eight basic melodies, put together in different ways. "There's no such thing as a new melody," he told a reporter. "My work is to connect the old phrases in a new way."

But new or old, Berlin's tunes catch on. Although most of his songs have been written for Tin Pan Alley—the commercial popular-song business—he has also written the scores for many successful musical comedies, including *Annie Get Your Gun* and *Call Me Madam*. And the melodies from those shows have taken their place alongside such old Berlin favorites as "Always" and "Alexander's Ragtime Band."

Berlin has made a fortune from his songs, too. In addition to royalties from the music he has written, he has shared in the profits from his successful stage ventures (including motion-picture rights: $650,000 for *Annie Get Your Gun*), and he has an income from his music publishing business as well. Since Berlin, publisher, handles the songs of Berlin, composer, he cannot lose!

Irving Berlin's success story is another of those which could happen only in America. He knows it and is the first to admit his debt of gratitude to the United States. That is why so much of his work has a sincere patriotic feeling, such as that in "God Bless America."

He was born in Siberia in 1888. One of eight children of Russian Jewish parents, he was named Israel Baline. His parents were forced to flee their home after a pogrom—one of those violent anti-Semitic outbursts with which Europe used to be plagued. When young "Izzy" was only four, they set out for America, in the hope of finding refuge.

They had no money and were ill-equipped for making

their way in a strange, new world. But at least they need not fear that their home would be burned as they slept, simply because their religion was different from that of the rulers. Papa Baline found an East Side tenement flat for his family in New York, and a job for himself as a Kosher meat inspector. They were poor but happy.

The elder Baline was a cantor in his spare time, singing at synagogues and temples. And since Izzy had a clear soprano voice, he learned his first music from his father.

But when Izzy was only eight years old, his father died, and the family went from poverty to desperation. All the children used to be sent out to raise money by doing odd jobs, and they would return at sundown to pool their earnings. Mrs. Baline had brought with her a brass samovar from Russia, and when things got too tough, she'd remove bits and pieces from the huge urn and sell them for bread money.

Years later Berlin said, "I never felt poverty because I'd never known anything else." Recalling that he used to sleep on fire escapes in the summertime, he said: "I slept better then than I do now in a bed!"

By the time he was fourteen, he was on his own. He made his first money by leading Blind Sol, a beggar, through the streets of the Bowery, and singing for tips when he got a chance. From here he drifted into singing in saloons, and plugging songs at famous old Tony Pastor's Café. He never made more than five dollars a week until he finally landed a steady job as a singing waiter at the Pelham Café. Here he was paid the magnificent sum of seven dollars a week, plus tips—but he had to work all night, from eight till six.

The Pelham was a Chinatown restaurant, much publicized in its day as the hangout of thieves and cutthroats. It is probable that this legend was built up to encourage the tourist trade, however. It apparently worked, too. For one of the Pelham's distinguished visitors was Prince Louis of Battenburg, and Izzy Baline landed in the newspaper columns by refusing a tip from the prince.

According to Alexander Woollcott, Berlin lost this job in 1907 because he fell asleep one night while in charge of the cash register. He immediately got another job, however, at Jimmy Kelly's in Union Square. And it was here that he introduced his first published song: "Marie from Sunny Italy."

Today we think of Berlin as a writer of both words and music, but it is interesting to note that he began as a lyricist. The music of "Marie" was by another singing waiter, and Berlin realized all of thirty-seven cents in royalties from this first effort.

He next wrote a lyric for a vaudeville performer, a song-and-dance man who wanted something topical. The song was all about Dorando, an Italian marathon runner making headlines at the time. For some reason, the vaudevillian turned it down, and Berlin promptly took it to a publisher. The great man looked it over. "How does the melody go?" he asked.

Berlin hadn't thought of a melody, but he sat down at once and improvised a tune. The publisher bought it for twenty-five dollars! On the strength of this success, Berlin left Chinatown and the Bowery and became a full-time staff lyricist for the publishing house, at twenty-five dollars a week. He was on his way.

Soon he was writing songs that were selling 300,000 to 500,000 copies, and his course was set. With "Alexander's

Ragtime Band" in 1911, he hit the top and remained there.

"Alexander's Ragtime Band" is more than just a song hit. Although it was not a show tune, it deserves more than passing mention here because of what it represents. Until then, much of the music being written by American popular composers was sentimental, trite, and uninspired. Few Americans were trying to develop anything new, anything truly native to America. There had been some cakewalks, coon-shouts, and low-down blues in the early minstrel shows, but there had been no attempt to make popular music out of the ragtime and "jazz" being heard in places like New Orleans.

How a Russian-born cantor's son from the Lower East Side managed to capture this catchy new American music is one of the mysteries of all time. But capture it he did, and with it the hearts of all Americans. They loved "Alexander's Ragtime Band" and demanded more. It can be said that this song, more than any other, changed the whole character of American popular music. Gershwin was to progress even further in the same direction, and such men as Youmans and Porter refined and clarified the new mood. But Berlin is almost certainly the man who set it.

The song was introduced by none other than George M. Cohan, in the Friars' Frolics of 1911. But it quickly drifted out of this inner sanctum of Broadway into the dance halls and places of amusement where people were beginning to demand lively tunes. Within a short time, "Alexander's Ragtime Band" was a tremendous hit. Berlin was made a full partner in the publishing house, and the jazz age was beginning to blossom into being.

The following year, Berlin married Dorothy Goetz and

they went to Cuba on a honeymoon. While there she contracted typhoid fever, and five months later she was dead. It was a terrible tragedy for the young composer. Out of the depths of his emotion he wrote a song, "When I Lost You," which is among the finest of his works. Perhaps the song was also a turning point in his career. Up to that time he had concentrated on catchy dance tunes. He had never tried to put his feelings into a song. "When I Lost You" broke down the last barriers of emotional reserve and allowed him to write the more sentimental tunes as well.

In the meantime, however, Berlin had made his bow as a stage composer. To be sure, at first he contributed only occasional numbers for revues, and thus had to meet none of the requirements of plot and character. But he was acquiring the kind of experience which would stand him in good stead in later years, when "show business" was to occupy so much of his time.

In 1914 he undertook to write the entire score for a musical, *Watch Your Step*. Although he wrote his own lyrics, the book was by that dependable librettist, Harry B. Smith, who had written *Robin Hood* with De Koven and *The Fortune Teller* with Victor Herbert. Described as a "syncopated musical show," *Watch Your Step* capitalized on the dance craze then sweeping the country. It was so successful that one critic wrote: "Berlin is now part of America."

With other composers, Berlin contributed bits and parts of other shows, too. In 1916 he wrote some of the music for *The Century Girl;* Victor Herbert did the rest of it. In 1918 he shared honors with George M. Cohan for the last of *The Cohan Revues*. That same year he joined forces with John Philip Sousa, famous American bandmaster and composer of "The Stars and Stripes Forever," to provide music for a spectacle called *Everything*.

On this occasion, the lyricist was John Golden, better known in later years as a producer of plays, but no mean song-writer himself. In his autobiography, *Stage-Struck John Golden,* the author described what it was like to work with Irving Berlin. They labored steadily from seven to eleven P. M. just to finish one song. Then Berlin said, "Let's try it again."

Before Golden could stop him he was off on an entirely new approach to the same song. At one A. M. this was finished, and Golden was ready to quit. But not Berlin. He wanted a third version, so they could choose the best one!

As Golden put it: "Irving Berlin may be a genius but that isn't the only reason he is one of the most successful composers today. Whatever Irving Berlin has reaped, he has earned; and I'm here to testify to it."

Berlin himself has admitted that hard work is far more important than "genius." "I was born with a first-rate talent," he says, "and the rest has been energy."

Like another composer, Richard Rodgers, he has to go looking for tunes. "It's not inspiration with me," he once said. "Generally I decide in a very prosaic way that I'm going to write something and then I sit down and do it." He usually starts with a word-phrase first, repeats it over and over until it creates a sort of basic rhythm, then develops it into a tune.

When the United States entered World War I, Berlin was drafted. Newspapers put it in headlines: "U.S. Takes Berlin."

At Camp Upton he wrote a musical show called *Yip, Yip, Yaphank,* which was presented on Broadway. This contribution to morale was just one of Sergeant Berlin's patriotic services to his country. In the show he sang, "Oh, How I Hate to Get Up in the Morning!" Soldiers and civilians have been singing it ever since.

For the finale of *Yaphank,* Berlin wrote a stirring song called "God Bless America," but for some reason it was discarded and never sung in public until twenty years later, when America stood on the brink of another World War. In this second conflict, "God Bless America" was a sort of theme song. It was sung by all our allies. When Mac Arthur returned to the Philippines and the Stars and Stripes were raised over the city, Filipino youngsters sang "God Bless America" in the streets.

Berlin assigned all royalties from this song to the Boy and Girl Scouts of America. By 1954 these royalties amounted to over $150,000, and were still climbing.

Berlin made another contribution to morale during the first World War. But he did it indirectly, through another composer, and he didn't even know about it until years later.

One of his early songs was "If I Had My Way, I'd Live Among the Gypsies." It was never very popular, but Berlin used to sing it occasionally in public. Among those who heard the song was Cole Porter, not yet a famous composer but a youngster fresh from Yale. He memorized the song, and later, when called upon to entertain troops at the front, he sang it.

The song caught on. It became especially popular among World War I fliers of the Ninety-Fourth or Hat-in-the-Ring Squadron, commanded by Captain Eddie Rickenbacker. Today many a veteran grows more sentimental about this Berlin tune than any other he wrote—thanks to the "plugging" of a rival composer.

After the war, Berlin returned to civilian life. In 1919 he established the firm of Irving Berlin, Inc., to publish popular songs. By now he was so successful that he could afford to pay $2,600 for a forty-volume set of Shakespeare!

He had long dreamed of building a theater which would be dedicated to musical comedy and revues alone. In partnership with two other East Side boys, Sam Harris and Joseph M. Schenck, he purchased a valuable Manhattan property and built the Music Box Theater at a cost of nearly a million dollars. The first *Music Box Revue,* which opened the theater in 1921, cost over $188,000—a fabulous amount for those days—and friends prophesied disaster.

They were wrong. The revue was such a success that it ran for 313 performances and made $400,000 in clear profits. Subsequent *Music Box Revues* were equally successful, featuring such stars as Fannie Brice, Grace Moore, and Bobby Clark. These annual revues were not continued after 1924, but the Music Box remained in business.

In all of these ventures, however, Berlin's musical contributions were little different from the popular songs he had been writing all along. They seldom had to meet the requirements of a story. They were "occasional" melodies, as distinguished from the later "show tunes" he was to write.

In 1925 he did write the score for a musical comedy of sorts. It was *The Cocoanuts,* featuring the zany Marx Brothers. These comics paid so little attention to plot and lines, however, that the show might more aptly be described as another revue.

That same year Berlin wrote two other tunes that were to overshadow by far anything he wrote for Groucho Marx and his playful relatives. These were "All Alone" and "Always"—

two of the most enduring love songs in the entire popular library. They had a special meaning for Berlin, because he was in love with Ellin Mackay, the lovely daughter of the head of Postal Telegraph, a social registerite, and a woman of great charm.

Berlin's suit was successful. When the two were married, the event made headlines throughout the country. And Irving Berlin gave his wife as a wedding gift the rights to "Always"—a typically sentimental touch from a man who lived by sentiment.

The great depression hit Berlin, like almost everyone else in show business. But he had known tough times before, and he knew how to work hard. He went about the business of recouping a lost fortune. Fortunately people still wanted to sing and to be entertained. During the depression years, Berlin made a million dollars in royalties, thanks to diligent application of the fingers to the keyboard.

The keyboard, in this case, is that of a piano equipped with a strange contraption which automatically transposes whatever Berlin writes to any key he desires. Since he can play in only one key—F sharp—this mechanism, which he calls his "Buick," is virtually indispensable.

With *Face the Music* in 1932, Berlin joined forces with one of the theater's ablest satirists, Moss Hart. While this again was a revue, it was more than a mere procession of vaudeville acts and spectacles. It had something sharp to say about political corruption, depression, and the sad state of the world. But it said these things brightly and entertainingly, and Berlin's music was an integral part of the whole scheme. Two tunes from this show are still heard: "Soft Lights and Sweet Music" and "Let's Have Another Cup of Coffee."

Following the success of this venture, Berlin and Hart teamed up on a second, called *As Thousands Cheer*. By all accounts this must have been just about the liveliest, most hilarious revue ever staged! It featured such performers as Clifton Webb and Ethel Waters, and such hit songs as "Not for All the Rice in China," and "The Easter Parade." Again the Berlin words and music were vital to the success of the whole enterprise. The show was produced in 1933, at the height of the depression, and it was an immense success.

For several years after this Broadway hit, Berlin devoted most of his time to writing for film musicals. All America was soon humming and whistling such sprightly tunes as "Cheek to Cheek," "Top Hat, White Tie and Tails," and "I've Got My Love to Keep Me Warm." These tunes were popularized by Ginger Rogers and Fred Astaire, but there was another movie tune which was to last even longer.

It was, of course, "White Christmas"—from a Bing Crosby movie called *Holiday Inn*. Berlin had long had the idea of writing a popular song for every American holiday. He was already one up with "The Easter Parade." Hollywood gave him free rein and the result was *Holiday Inn*—not too good a picture, according to the critics, but popular with fans of both Crosby and Berlin.

Berlin returned to Broadway in 1940 with *Louisiana Purchase*. Then came the second World War and the call of duty. He composed a song called "Any Bonds Today?" which was used to help sell War Bonds to the public. But his greatest contribution was another all-soldier show called *This Is the Army*. Produced on a much more lavish scale than *Yip, Yip, Yaphank*, it played throughout the country and in Europe, was later translated to the screen. Altogether *This Is the Army* netted over ten million dollars, which was distributed among the various relief agencies of the Armed Forces.

After the show opened, Berlin asked a Philadelphia audience what song they would like to hear. Their answer was "Praise the Lord and Pass the Ammunition!" which was then a popular wartime song. It happened to be written by another composer, Frank Loesser, but Berlin sang it anyway. Afterward he chuckled: "If I had refused, they would have said I am jealous. Now I suppose they'll say I tried to claim I wrote it!"

After the war he wrote *Miss Liberty* with Robert E. Sherwood, the distinguished American dramatist who was taking a fling at musical comedy. This show, though successful, was outclassed by a later Berlin effort: *Annie Get Your Gun.*

It is interesting to note that *Annie* had originally been intended for Jerome Kern, but upon his death, the assignment was given to Berlin. The show was produced by Rodgers and Hammerstein and featured Ethel Merman. It ran for three years in New York and was considered Berlin's greatest Broadway success.

Here the music had to fit the plot, and it did, beautifully, in such numbers as "Doin' What Comes Natcherly," "They Say It's Wonderful," and "The Girl that I Marry." With *Annie* Irving Berlin achieved his full stature as a composer of musical comedy.

His next effort, also for Ethel Merman, was *Call Me Madam,* a gentle satire on the life of a lady diplomat. Also an outstanding success, it was equally popular as a motion picture.

Berlin soon set to work on a film, *White Christmas,* featuring that old favorite and some new tunes. And Broadway awaited word of his next stage production. Late in 1953 the papers made note of the fact that one Linda Berlin, daughter of Irving and Ellin Berlin, was making her stage debut. And Broadway observers were betting that this is the production of which Irving Berlin is proudest!

George Gershwin

"All I've got is a lot of talent and plenty of nerve."

So said George Gershwin, summing up his musical career. The words, as far as they go, are quite true—except that the *talent* may be better described as genius and the *nerve* as a restless, inquiring nature.

It is a good thing for Americans that Gershwin was restless and ambitious. Otherwise he might have left behind a much smaller body of work when he died at the very prime of life—aged thirty-nine. As it is, we have such towering contributions as "Rhapsody in Blue," "An American in Paris," and *Porgy and Bess,* plus an almost endless procession of lighter but no less artful works, such as "I Got Rhythm," "Embraceable You," "Lady Be Good," and so on.

You can scarcely listen to music at all without hearing Gershwin at one time or another. His American folk-opera, *Porgy and Bess,* enjoyed its second Broadway revival in 1953, almost twenty years after its first production. His *Of Thee I Sing,* the first musical comedy ever to win a Pulitzer Prize, was a Broadway hit again two decades after its first New York bow. Annually his works are played at a Gershwin Memorial Concert at Lewissohn Stadium, New York. And the chances are that you hum or whistle some of them yourself.

Actually Gershwin was being modest when he said he had "a lot of talent." Yet modesty was not a virtue for which he was noted. Those who knew him and loved him grew to accept his profound interest in himself as something quite natural. Actually, he saw no reason to pose; he was always completely open and frank. There was no point in pretending that the work of George Gershwin did not interest George Gershwin more than anything else in the world.

He once said of *Porgy and Bess,* "The music is so marvelous I really can't believe I wrote it!" This remark, coming from a less gifted composer than Gershwin, might be unpardonable. But it was part of his innocent, trusting nature to say such things in complete sincerity, never dreaming that anyone would misconstrue them.

His good friend, pianist Oscar Levant, once asked him, "George, if you had it to do all over again, would you still fall in love with yourself?"

And Gershwin could laugh at this impudence, too.

Once Gershwin's mother took him to task because he always played his own music at parties. "But, Mama," he answered, "I don't have a good time unless I'm playing." And it was perfectly true. He was at his best when seated before a keyboard, playing his own music. Otherwise he was inclined to get restless and bored.

His brother Ira, with whom he wrote almost every one of his successful musical comedies, says that this was because George was essentially a shy, retiring man with a great deal of reserve. Music broke down this reserve to some extent, allowed him to relax and have a good time.

As a boy, Gershwin was much more interested in baseball and girls than in music. Born in Brooklyn in 1898, he had a typical childhood. He was no genius at school, had no particular interest in books, and scorned music as a waste of time.

At the age of ten, when he was attending Public School 25, one of his schoolmates was Maxie Rosenzweig (who later became Max Rosen, celebrated violinist). One day Maxie was giving a concert in the school auditorium and George was outside playing ball. Suddenly he was arrested by the strains of Dvořák's "Humoresque" floating through the open window. For some reason the music impressed young George, and he determined to make friends with Maxie.

He did, and the acquaintanceship opened up a whole new world of interest to Gershwin. Some time later George showed Maxie a few early attempts at writing music and the violinist said: "You have no talent for composition. Better forget about it."

Such advice was no deterrent to young George. Instead it merely set his determination harder. He was not afraid of hard work, particularly if there was a challenge involved. So George got busy. He studied serious music with an analytical mind. He took Bach's "The Well-Tempered Clavier" apart to see what made it tick. Perhaps it was just curiosity at first, or the desire to prove his friend Maxie wrong. But music soon took hold of him, with the result that before he was twenty years old he had one hit song to his credit and was making his living as a musician.

George's inquiring mind never deserted him. Even at the

height of his successful career, he continued to study Bach's fugues. He wanted to take lessons from the great French composer, Ravel. Ravel is said to have countered: "You are now writing first-rate Gershwin. If you study with me, it won't be long before you'll be writing second-rate Ravel!"

A similar exchange has been recorded between Gershwin and Stravinsky. George asked the Russian to tutor him in composition. Stravinsky replied: "How much money do you make a year, Mr. Gershwin?"

"About a hundred thousand dollars," George answered.

"Then I think you had better teach *me* composition!"

But we are getting ahead of our story. Let us go back to George's meeting with Maxie Rosenzweig and his awakened interest in music. Soon after this meeting, he persuaded his family to buy a piano, and it was on this instrument that he first picked out the popular tunes of the day. In fact, George was such a tireless piano thumper that his mother had to impose an eleven P. M. curfew so the family could get some sleep.

Later he studied piano with Charles Hambitzer and acquired the technique which was so evident whenever he performed. He entered one of Rubin Goldmark's composition classes and studied harmony with Edward Kilenyi. But on the whole, George's music was self-acquired. His natural curiosity, his determination to find out the why and wherefore led him quite naturally to composition.

The first song he wrote was something called "When You Want 'Em You Can't Get 'Em." Although the five dollars he got for it didn't go far, the prestige of being a popular song writer did. Others of his works were soon being noticed by such rising young stars as Vivienne Segal, for instance, who introduced a couple of his songs to a Sunday-night audience at the Century Theater.

Eventually he took a job as pianist in a music-publishing house. In those days song-pluggers operated much differently from today. Now a song-plugger spends most of his time being nice to radio disc jockeys or singing stars of the theater and television, hoping that they will give his songs a performance before a nationwide audience. Publication may or may not follow.

But in 1916 or thereabouts, when George went to work, things were different. The staff pianist in a publishing house was there to play the songs of aspiring composers for the publishers or anyone else who would listen. If a song sounded good to this small but select audience, it might then be published in the hope that the public would buy it. As a staff pianist, George had little chance for originality. He merely played other men's songs—good ones and bad ones alike.

But Max Dreyfuss, of the T. B. Harms Company, a large music-publishing house, thought he saw possibilities in this brilliant, ambitious youngster. So he said, "I'll gamble on you. I'll give you thirty-five dollars a week without any set duties. Just step in every morning and say hello. The rest will follow."

It did not take long to prove Dreyfuss's judgment correct. When Gershwin, free to compose his own music, turned out the hit song "Swanee," which the great Al Jolson made popular, the royalties started rolling in. And they have never stopped.

By the time he was twenty-one, Gershwin had written his first musical comedy: *La, La, Lucille.* It was a respectable enough attempt, but Gershwin was new at the business, and in spite of his enormous talent, he had a great deal to learn about writing for the theater. It was four and a half years before he tried again.

Meantime he continued to make his living as a pianist. Among other things, he was for a time accompanist for Nora Bayes, one of the most popular singers of the World War I era. It was at this time (around 1918) that Oscar Levant first became aware of Gershwin's talents.

But when Levant congratulated Gershwin on his work with Nora Bayes, George laughed. "She always said my playing took her mind off her work," he confessed. He added that she often threatened to fire him!

But Nora Bayes, one of the great names of stage music, was also responsible for launching the career of another member of the Gershwin family: George's older brother Ira. It was Ira with whom George was to write almost all his musical comedies, but back in the early days Ira was so modest about his own talents that he actually wrote his first song under a pseudonym: Arthur Francis (a combination of his brother's and sister's names). The song was called "The Real American Folk Song is a Rag," and Nora Bayes chose to include it in her act.

From 1920 to 1925 George and Ira wrote the music and lyrics for the annual George White's *Scandals*. In the meantime, Ira did one show, *Two Little Girls in Blue,* with Vincent Youmans. And George wrote the historic "Rhapsody in Blue" for a Paul Whiteman jazz concert.

Whiteman, sometimes known as "Pops" because of the many great musical stars whose careers he fathered—Bing Crosby, among others—had long had it in his mind to present a really important concert of jazz music. He felt, as did

Gershwin, that this new music was truly American, and that it deserved dignified attention from critics and the public.

Finally Whiteman decided to do something about it. He engaged Aeolian Hall, one of New York's best concert halls, and started preparing for the concert. But word of his plans leaked out and the idea of a jazz concert seemed such a good one that another popular orchestra leader of the day decided to put on his own show. The only way to keep him from grabbing the spotlight was to be first; so Whiteman had to move fast.

For that reason, Gershwin's jazz rhapsody—the major work of the program—had to be written, orchestrated, rehearsed and ready to perform within the short space of twenty-four days. Considering that many symphonies and other orchestral works take years to complete, twenty-four days was nothing! The work of supplying separate parts for each instrument in a huge symphony orchestra is in itself a gigantic task. For a composition of these dimensions, the time was frighteningly short. The music was totally new and unfamiliar, too, and the proper shading and interpretation required long hours of study and practice. But with Whiteman standing by, Gershwin finished the colossal job on time.

He later said that he conceived the whole work on a train ride to Boston, actually composed it on the upright piano in a back room at his parents' apartment. It had to be orchestrated a sheet at a time as he completed it, yet it was so nearly perfect that not a note of it was ever changed!

The night of the performance, with Gershwin at the piano, Whiteman, who was conducting, was so overcome with emotion that his eyes filled with tears. He says now that he doesn't know how he ever conducted the Rhapsody that night, for he woke up "eleven pages later" as though from a trance.

The Rhapsody won great acclaim, not only from the public but from the critics as well. Great names in the musical world heard that first performance, and all of them applauded the young composer. But Gershwin was not satisfied. When Whiteman heard this, he exploded: "Why, that damned fool! He thinks he can improve it!"

But Gershwin's reaction was perfectly typical. Oscar Levant tells about the time a friend came backstage after a performance to congratulate Gershwin. "The music was wonderful, George!"

"Is that all?" Gershwin answered. "Just wonderful?"

Stories like these were innumerable, for Gershwin had a real hunger for praise. He wanted people to tell him that his work was good; yet he himself was never satisfied. His brother Ira understood this better than anyone else.

When the two were working on a show, George was fast to act on flashes of inspiration. He never spared himself when the mood to compose was on him, and this as much as anything else may have shortened his life. Ira, on the other hand, was patient, careful, and painstaking. He was usually about three songs behind George.

But Ira's words so well suited George's music that their collaboration was entirely successful. Starting with *Lady, Be Good* in 1924, the two brothers had a dozen shows on Broadway in the next half-dozen years. These included *Oh, Kay; Funny Face; Strike Up the Band;* and *Girl Crazy*. Some of the brightest stars on Broadway helped to make these musicals memorable. Fred Astaire and his sister Adele dancing to Gershwin's smooth rhythms; Ethel Merman shouting his catchy tunes; Gertrude Lawrence, Victor Moore, and dozens of others. Few who heard it will ever forget Miss Merman's electrifying rendition of "I Got Rhythm."

Then came *Of Thee I Sing,* and musical comedy in America had suddenly taken a brand-new turn. Produced in 1931 at the height of the depression, this tuneful satire was the first musical comedy to stimulate the mind as well as the senses. Written by George S. Kaufman and Morrie Ryskind, *Of Thee I Sing* followed their earlier attempt at political satire, *Strike Up the Band,* with a really telling blow. The George Gershwin music and the Ira Gershwin lyrics were pointed, witty, and completely in harmony. *Of Thee I Sing* was a hit of really major proportions.

It was followed two years later by the less successful *Let 'Em Eat Cake,* but this was George's last musical comedy. *Porgy and Bess,* which appeared in 1935, is usually called an American folk opera. It differs from the rest of Gershwin's stage music as much as the "Rhapsody in Blue" differs from "Indian Love Call."

Gershwin chose for the libretto of his opera the poignant tale of a Negro in Charleston, South Carolina, whom the reading public had first met in Du Bose Heyward's novel, *Porgy.* Heyward was himself a poet, and his enthusiasm for Gershwin's project resulted in one of the most effective collaborations in theatrical history. The sensitive, tragic story, highlighted by such songs as "Summertime," "I Got Plenty of Nuthin'," and "Bess, You Is My Woman Now," remains a favorite with theater-goers.

Soon after *Porgy and Bess,* Gershwin went to Hollywood, where he and Ira worked on three screen musicals: *Shall We Dance, A Damsel in Distress,* and *Goldwyn Follies.* From this period at least two songs have survived: "Love Walked In," and "Our Love Is Here to Stay."

The movies have made much of Gershwin, however. A few years after his death they made a highly fictitious film biography of the composer. The movie was tremendously popular, but chiefly because of the fine renditions of some of his best works. Later *An American in Paris* borrowed the title of one of his symphonic poems, written in Paris in 1928, and allowed the agile Gene Kelly to dance to its music.

George never married. He died in Hollywood in 1937, after being stricken with a brain tumor. In spite of his untimely death, however, he had already won for himself a permanent place in American music. His brother Ira has continued to blend his own talents with those of other composers.

There was always a very close family feeling among the Gershwins. George adored his mother. He once said: "My mother's what the mammy writers write about and what the mammy singers sing about. But they don't mean it, and I do."

His father, too, held a warm spot in the affections of his family and friends. The elder Gershwin was noted for his unconscious humor. Once when he and George were in the Harms offices, they encountered Lou Hirsch, whose "Love Nest" was then a hit song. Hirsch proudly showed them a check for $26,000, first quarter's royalties on the song. "Papa" Gershwin took a look, seized the successful composer's hand and said sympathetically, "Good luck, Mr. Hirsch."

Another time George commented on a new paper by Albert Einstein, the great mathematician. "Imagine working for twenty years and putting your results into three pages!" he said.

"Papa" thought this one over. Then he said slowly, "Well, it was probably very small print."

But it was George himself about whom most stories were told.

His good friend Kay Swift recalled a party at which some musical friends were gathered. As usual George managed to get to the piano, where he played for better than an hour, completely relaxed and at ease. Suddenly he jumped up and said, "I have to go to Europe!" Whereupon he rushed out of the house and barely made the boat.

Once he told Rouben Mamoulian not to apologize for arriving at a dinner party unshaven. "Personally, I love you that way."

Mamoulian asked him why. "Because then you look like me," Gershwin answered.

Alexander Woollcott used to tell a story about George and Harry Ruby, another song writer. The two were playing ball together when George quit to protect his hands. Ruby was indignant: "What about *my* hands?"

"Well, it's not the same thing," George replied.

Ruby, none too happy at this exchange, didn't see Gershwin again for a couple of years. When he did, he reminded Gershwin of the incident.

"Well," said George, "it *isn't* the same thing."

Woollcott is also responsible for the story about a former girl friend of Gershwin's. Someone told George that she had married someone else. His answer was, "I'd feel terrible about this if I weren't so busy right now."

But if these tales, true or not, seem to add up to an egotistical, selfish man, they give a mistaken impression. For George was always modest, always certain his work could be better, always conscious of his debt to such men as Kilenyi and Goldmark. He happened to find his work—his music—more fascinating than anything else in the world, and he saw no reason to hide this.

If he had loved it less, perhaps we should not love it so much.

VINCENT YOUMANS

THERE is tragedy in the story of Vincent Youmans. It is the tragedy of a man who died too young, who fought a losing battle against tuberculosis, and who was unhappy and dissatisfied with the work he did.

There is irony in the story, too. For despite Youmans' scorn for the popular success of his music, much of that music will endure longer than the serious compositions he so much preferred.

Vincent Youmans died an unhappy man; but he left the world some of the happiest music it has ever heard. "Hallelujah!" for instance, and "Rise 'n' Shine" are two of the liveliest, peppiest tunes ever written. "Tea for Two" and "Drums in My Heart" are equally bright and optimistic.

Youmans could be sentimental, too, and reflective, as witness "Time on My Hands" and "More than You Know." But these unforgettable songs were, to him, only a compromise with the artistic standards he had set for himself.

His tragedy is that he never attained those standards. His

triumph is that he came so close, without ever realizing it.

Youmans drifted into the theater almost by accident. He was born in New York in 1898, of English-Irish parentage. His father was a prosperous hatter who dictated the styles of men's silk hats and derbies and the "proper shapes in ladies' round hats, bonnets, and walking hats." Young Vincent was at first destined for the same business.

By the time he could walk, however, he was interested in music. At the age of four, his training began. He was given lessons by Charles André Feller, organist of the First Methodist Episcopal Church of New Rochelle, New York.

While his family approved, there was no thought of music as a career for the lad. His mother felt that the ability to play the piano was a pleasant social grace, but little more. His early musical training was along formal and classical lines, and he continued it through his years in school.

He attended Trinity School in Mamaroneck, a suburban New York community, and later went to preparatory school at Heathcote Hall, Rye, New York. Far from planning a musical career, Youmans expected to enter the famed Sheffield School of Engineering at Yale, where an uncle had distinguished himself.

But in the summer of his seventeenth year, as World War I brewed in Europe, he took a job in a brokerage house in Wall Street. He liked the work, and the firm apparently liked him; so he decided to give up Yale and engineering in favor of a career in finance. But this was not to be. When America entered the war in 1917, Youmans resigned his position and enlisted in the Navy.

At the Great Lakes Naval Training Station, where he was first assigned, his musical talent was soon discovered. Before he knew it, Youmans had been assigned to an entertainment unit. He had joined the Navy to see the world, but he never got out of the country. Instead he fought his war from a bandstand, at the piano bench, and in the wings of many an improvised stage.

The head bandmaster at the Station was John Philip Sousa, the March King, composer of "The Stars and Stripes Forever." Youmans showed some of his tunes to the great man. Sousa liked one of them very much, had it scored for band instruments, and passed it along to other Navy bands. The tune had no name then, but nine years later it swept the country as "Hallelujah!"

If it had not been for the war and Youmans' Navy experience, he might never have turned his attention to music of the popular type. But with his background as composer and producer of wartime sailor shows, it was only natural that his first job after the war should be with a music publishing house.

A staff pianist, Youmans' chief job was as song-plugger. In other words, he was employed to sell the songs of other composers—a chore which many of the brightest names in musical comedy have undertaken at one time or another. But Youmans had an additional duty, and one that gave him an added advantage in the race for prominence. He was hired to rehearse singers for Victor Herbert shows.

Youmans said later that this was the most valuable experience he ever had. "There are no treatises or instruction books," he told a reporter, "on how to write an opera or musical comedy, so I was fortunate to work with a man like Herbert. I got something in less than a year that money could not buy."

Along about this time Youmans wrote his first "hit" song. It was called "Who's Who with You," and it appeared in the musical show, *Piccadilly to Broadway*. Aside from its place in the record, however, it has little importance.

Youmans was then twenty-two years old, and had embarked on a career that was to bring him fame and fortune. But he did not regard his new work in that light. Instead he looked on it as merely a stopgap, a pleasant enough interlude—but only an interlude—in the study and production of symphonies, oratorios, and operas. He was to hold that view through the next dozen years—the most productive in his life.

It is probably because of this rather patronizing attitude toward musical comedy songs that Youmans got the reputation of being aloof and withdrawn. Many of those who worked with him in the theater of the 1920's felt that he was holding back, never giving all he had to give, hoarding his talents. Some accused him of coldness, of egotism, of consuming ambition.

A small, dark man with a handsome, brooding face, he was not easy to like. Yet he had a host of friends among those who knew the workings of his mind. And everyone, friend or enemy, had to concede that here was one of the most brilliant talents in America, a talent that not even his own indifference could hide.

In later years, when his failing health forced him to be away from New York for extended periods of time, the legend of Youmans' aloofness grew. These prolonged absences, coupled with his increasing interest in the study of serious music, made him seem something of a hermit to those who remained on Broadway and visited the clubs, cafés, and theaters regularly.

Perhaps the reason for the legend is that Youmans was an introvert. Shyness prevented him from making friends readily, but those who knew his brilliant mind, his lofty ambitions, and his disappointments felt that he was a man well worth knowing.

In his early years in the theater, however, few could have suspected that Youmans was to flash across the sky like a meteor and fade as quickly. After that first hit song in 1920, his progress seemed steady and sure. In 1921, for instance, his first full musical comedy score was presented on Broadway. It was *Two Little Girls in Blue,* with lyrics by Ira Gershwin. In the next decade, Youmans was to write no less than ten hit shows.

The first of these was *Wildflower,* with Otto Harbach and Oscar Hammerstein II as librettists. Only one song from this show has remained popular—"Bambolina." But *Wildflower* deserved its success if only because the score was a more varied and colorful one than those of most of the musical comedies of the day.

The next year came *No, No, Nanette!* probably one of the most successful musical comedies ever produced. In a day when long-run musicals were a rarity (for there were many more each season than there are now), it lasted for a year in New York and for almost two years in London. Seventeen road companies played it in various parts of the world—Europe, South America, China, New Zealand, the Philippines, and Java. It earned Vincent Youmans half a million dollars and a permanent—if unwanted—place in American musical comedy.

By today's standards, *No, No, Nanette!* seems old-fashioned, and its popularity hard to understand. But two of its songs,

"Tea for Two" and "I Want to Be Happy," still have the power to move listeners with their charm and simplicity. Perhaps it was that same quality of charm and simplicity which gave the show its enormous appeal.

Another Youmans success arrived in 1926. It was *Oh, Please!* starring Beatrice Lillie and Charles Winninger. "I Know that You Know" was the best song from this score, and again audiences were treated to that vigorous, driving rhythm that characterizes so many of Youmans' songs. Listening to such songs, and recalling how many years they have remained "standards" in the popular music field, one feels Youmans' personal tragedy even more intensely.

With the success of *No, No, Nanette!* he had grown ambitious to produce as well as compose his own shows. With *Hit the Deck* in 1927, he achieved that ambition. Reminiscent of his early days in the Navy, *Hit the Deck* was a musical about sailors and their girls. With the aid of "Hallelujah" and "Sometimes I'm Happy," the new show struck the popular fancy and its music was heard all over the country.

About this time Youmans married Anne Varley, a dancer. This marriage, though happy at first, was not destined to last. Youmans' growing discontent with the work he was doing, his driving ambition, and other problems of temperament and disposition led to divorce in 1933—but not until after twin children had been born.

Youmans remarried in 1935, but was again divorced, shortly before his untimely death.

After his debut as a producer with *Hit the Deck,* Youmans presented another show, *Great Day,* which deserved better success than it won. An ambitious undertaking, presented at great cost, it never quite caught on with the public. But three songs from this show, with lyrics by Billy Rose, did catch on and are frequently heard today: "Great Day," "Without a Song," and "More than You Know."

Another venture, *Through the Years,* was a musical adaptation of the sentimental play, *Smilin' Through.* Again Youmans had overreached himself in production costs, and had tried to do too much of the work himself. The production lost money, but two of Youmans' songs, "Through the Years" and "Drums in My Heart," survived.

Youmans had only one more Broadway production: *Take a Chance,* in 1932. This musical was tailor-made for the talents of Ethel Merman, and it fit her like one of her own spangled sheaths. Youmans provided her with what Cecil Smith has described as "two of the best songs anyone ever wrote for an American musical comedy"—"Eadie Was a Lady," and "Rise 'n' Shine." The last-named song is still capable of bringing audiences to their feet shouting "bravo!"

In 1933 Youmans went to Hollywood, the inevitable destination of all successful composers of musical comedy. His first movie was the tremendously popular *Flying Down to Rio,* in which Ginger Rogers and Fred Astaire were teamed for the first time. "The Carioca" and "Orchids in the Moonlight" indicated once more that Youmans had one of the finest talents in America.

But now began for Vincent Youmans a bad time. He contracted tuberculosis and was forced to rest and to seek a more healthful climate. Friends said he almost welcomed the unlucky break. He had enough money, and now, for the first time, enough leisure, to devote himself to the study of serious music.

During the twelve years that followed, Youmans studied

and wrote. At Loyola University, in New Orleans, he enrolled in the music school to study harmony and instrumentation. He had long been interested, as a hobby, in liturgical music: the chants, responses, chorales, and other forms which developed in the church. At Loyola he had an opportunity to study this form of music—and incidentally to indulge his hobby of deep-sea fishing in the waters of the Gulf of Mexico.

Hospitalized for part of the time, he also wrote serious music: symphonies, fugues, cantatas, and so on. It is part of his tragedy that none of his serious music was published in his lifetime. Most of it has never been performed or heard publicly.

He did turn his thoughts, occasionally, to show music, too. He wrote and planned some musicals which he hoped to produce eventually. All of this music now rests in a New York bank vault.

His fight against the dread disease was a losing one. In and out of sanitariums, he made infrequent excursions back East, where he maintained a home in Westchester County, New York, and another on the New Jersey coast, for fishing.

In 1944 he made a final attempt to come back to the theater. With the reputed backing of Doris Duke, "richest girl in the world," he produced the Vincent Youmans Ballet Revue, which opened in Baltimore and toured the United States and Canada. However, the work never reached Broadway.

Doctors finally advised him to go to Colorado. Within a few weeks after his arrival, however, he died in his suite at a Denver hotel. At his bedside were Mary Chase, author of the prize-winning play, *Harvey,* and her husband, a Denver newspaperman and old friend of Youmans.

His body was brought back to New York for funeral services, at which Deems Taylor, famous American composer and then President of ASCAP, presided. The body was cremated and the ashes scattered in New York harbor near the Ambrose Light Vessel.

Youmans, who had never wanted musical comedy success, had won it in spite of himself. As Cecil Smith says, "His loss was a deprivation for the musical stage, for in his time he alone deserved to be ranked with Gershwin, Porter, Rodgers, and Kern." Other composers, the librettists and writers with whom he worked, as well as actors, producers, and theater people, echo these sentiments. They may never have understood the little dark fellow with the deep voice, but they recognized genius when they saw it.

COLE PORTER

EVEN if Cole Porter had written nothing else but "Night and Day," his fame would be perfectly secure. For that great song, composed in the early 1930's, is still fresh and new. Two generations of young people have sung its haunting melody and been stirred by its pulsing rhythms.

But Cole Porter has written more—so many more! "Begin the Beguine" and "I've Got You Under My Skin" for exotic rhythms; "You're the Top" and "Anything Goes" for tricky tunes and sophisticated rhymes; "Friendship" and "Don't Fence Me In" for pure comedy; "Wunderbar" and "I Love Paris" for romantic melody.

The list is almost endless, and as colorful and varied as a tray of Christmas cookies.

It is hard to realize that the same man could write songs of such opposite appeal as "An Old Fashioned Garden," with its frankly sentimental words and melody, and "Get Out of Town," in which the sentiment is approached from a ninety-degree angle.

But then, Cole Porter is a bit of a paradox himself. He has never had to work; yet he has been one of the most untiring of composers. He was born on an Indiana farm; yet he has spent much of his life abroad. His songs sound effortless and easy; yet they are artfully plotted and planned. His name is almost as well known as those of the stars he helped to make famous—Ethel Merman, Mary Martin, Danny Kaye; yet he could pass in any crowd unnoticed.

In appearance he is decidedly "average." Neither tall nor short, fat nor thin, dark nor light, he has a pleasant, amiable face, with only a slight suggestion of the pixie that sometimes creeps into his songs. When Ed Sullivan honored him in 1953 on a television show devoted to his music, one critic remarked that Porter looked as though he'd just drifted in from the string section of the orchestra.

But once he sets his agile mind to work, the results are far from "average." A Cole Porter song has such a distinctive flavor—whether it is a throbbing love song or a satirical ditty—that it cannot be mistaken.

The characteristic bolero rhythm of "Night and Day" is heard again in "I've Got You Under My Skin," "Begin the Beguine," and "What Is This Thing Called Love?" The witty lyrics of "You're the Top" are just as recognizable in "It's De-Lovely" and "Anything Goes."

The Porter stamp on a song is as plain as a trade mark.

It was not apparent, of course, in "The Bobolink Waltz," which was Porter's first composition. But then he was just a boy of eleven at the time. An Indiana boy, but hardly a Hoosier—at least not in the same sense as that other Indiana boy, Herb Shriner. For there was nothing homespun about Cole Porter, even then.

His family was well-to-do. His father owned a farm near Peru, Indiana, where Porter was born in 1893. His grandfather had made a fortune in West Virginia in timber and coal-mining. Even today, Cole Porter always wears white socks in memory of the old man, who left him a share in his seven-million-dollar fortune.

How much of farm life stuck with Porter it would be difficult to say. Certainly little of it is reflected in his songs. One of his sharpest satires, for instance, is a piece called "Farming," which was first sung by Danny Kaye in *Let's Face It,* and which makes great sport of the back-to-the-soil movement which was once fashionable among city dwellers.

But maybe a little of the good earth stuck to the boy, for he once told a reporter that he intended to spend his old age gardening—in his back yard in Paris, he added.

We do know that he met up with two loves in those early days which were to remain with him always: thoroughbred horses—and music. By the time he was six he had mastered the violin, the piano at eight. He had also learned how to ride.

After some early schooling at Peru, he was sent East to prep school at Worcester Academy in Massachusetts, and from there he moved on to Yale.

He had promised his grandfather that he would study law: that was one of the conditions of the inheritance. And he meant to do so, but he couldn't kill his love of music. At Yale in 1911 and 1912 he wrote two football songs: "Yale Bull Dog Song" and "Bingo Eli Yale"—both of which are still sung occasionally by the Whiffenpoofs, Yale's famous singing society.

At college he was a member of Scroll and Key, a campus

secret society. After meetings, the members were supposed to march in a body from their clubhouse to their places of residence. Instead, Porter always steered them—in a body—to the Taft Hotel to hear the dance band.

As a scholar, Porter was at least average. He had many other interests, however, and was considered by his classmates to be a lively, likeable fellow. After his graduation from Yale in 1913, he entered Harvard Law School, true to his promise to his grandfather.

But a persistent urge was upon him. It was the urge to write songs, and to know more about the fascinating world of music. He felt reasonably certain that his grandfather wouldn't understand or approve what he wanted to do. Rather than hurt the old man's feelings, Porter stuck it out at Law School for a year. But at the end of that time, he could no longer resist his musical ambitions. He transferred to the Harvard School of Music.

The reaction at home was immediate and automatic. Porter was cut out of his grandfather's will.

So the die was cast. Porter began to study harmony and counterpoint, the tools of the composer's trade. Before long he was experimenting with new harmonies and different rhythms. Finally, while still in the School of Music, he wrote his first musical comedy.

It was called *See America First,* and it concerned a young debutante who wanted to escape from the artificial world of society by living close to nature on a ranch. There she met a cowboy who, of course, turned out to be a duke. The story had elements of satire, and considerable wit, and the show was at least good enough to attract a Broadway producer.

However, it expired ingloriously after only fifteen performances. Porter's librettist entered the priesthood and Porter himself joined the French Foreign Legion!

This move was perfectly characteristic. Another young man, disinherited by his grandfather and disillusioned by his first failure, might have taken to drink, started a brand-new career, or hopped a train bound for California at the very most. But Porter did the most romantic, unlikely, and unconventional thing imaginable—he joined the French Foreign Legion.

The year was 1916 and Europe was at war, so Porter's move was more than just a gesture. It meant he would be actively engaged in the world combat before his own country had even entered.

It did not take the French long to discover that here was an American with great spirit, talent, and wit. Soon he was entertaining the troops with music and song—his own and that of other composers as well, including Irving Berlin, who, Porter says, is still his favorite composer. The story goes that he actually marched with a portable piano on his back! At any rate, he was always ready to perform, always cheerful, and always in the thick of things.

As evidence of this, the French government awarded him the *Croix de Guerre,* its treasured military decoration, for his morale-building services, his comradeship, and his personality in the first World War. Though intensely proud of this decoration, Porter modestly pooh-poohs his own accomplishments. "If I succeed in entertaining others," he says, "it's only because I'm forever trying to entertain myself."

It was during his wartime service that he wrote his first song hit. (Nothing from *See America First* caught on.) This was "An Old-Fashioned Garden," which is rarely heard today, but which old-timers remember as a fine song of the World War I era. Sentimental and unsophisticated, it was a far cry from the works which Porter was to produce later, but it did prove one thing: He had the gift of melody—the kind of melody that people remember.

After a period of service with the Foreign Legion, he transferred to the French Artillery, and when America entered the war he trained soldiers from the United States at the Artillery School at Fontainebleau. Sent to the front as a French officer, he remained in the thick of the fighting till the end of the war.

Meantime, in Paris, he had met a young American widow, Linda Lee Thomas, and after the Armistice he decided that he wanted to remain for a while in Paris. He undertook advanced studies at the Schola Cantorum, to acquire an even more solid grounding in the fundamentals of composition, harmony, and counterpoint.

But at last the young man felt that he must go home. He sailed for the United States with little notion of what he would do when he arrived there. Luckily he met Raymond Hitchcock, then a popular musical comedy star, who remembered some of the good things about *See America First.* Like other showmen, Hitchcock was always looking for fresh ideas, and in Cole Porter he found them. He commissioned Porter to write the music for his new revue, *Hitchy-Koo of 1919.*

According to one critic, this revue, which was one of a series featuring Hitchcock, was "Hitchier than ever in its fun, more Kooey than ever before in its music." The show ran for two years, during which time Porter continued to collect handsome royalties. His reputation was made, but what seemed more important at the time, he could return to Paris and Linda Lee Thomas.

That is exactly what he did do. He married Mrs. Thomas and they settled in Paris. After the success of Porter's *Hitchy-Koo* revue, his grandfather had decided that the boy would make good, law or no law, and had finally left him a share in the family fortune. So Porter was now independently wealthy, married to a wealthy wife, and living in Paris on a sizeable income.

The temptation to most men would have been to stop working. But Porter's restless nature, his constant wish to "entertain himself" would not let him stop. It is true that for a number of years he spent more time in Paris and the fashionable capitals of Europe than in the United States. It is also true that almost ten years passed before he had another solidly successful show to his credit. But Porter's mind was at work, even while he played. He was building the kind of experiences and the kind of perception that were to make his later shows so appealing.

Stories were told about the Porters. How they attended parties every night. How they had a home in Paris, a villa in Venice, an estate on the Riviera, a penthouse in New York. How they had decorated their home with platinum wallpaper and zebra-skin upholstery. How they hired fifty gondoliers to act as footmen, and an entire troupe of tightrope walkers plus the Monte Carlo ballet to entertain their party guests.

The stories persisted even after Porter was spending more and more time actively writing for the theater. Perhaps they added to the legend of the rich playboy and thus made his music more appealing to certain people; perhaps they are merely the exaggerations of columnists. At any rate, clear up to 1937, when Porter suffered a serious accident, the legend kept building. Then, in a mood to be serious, the public no longer heard about the playboy composer. Instead they heard about a gifted musician who was making a desperate fight for recovery and earnestly turning out musical scores. And it has been that way ever since, through successes and failures —with a heavy balance on the success side.

Whatever can be said about those years abroad, one thing is certain: we should probably never have had a "Night and Day" or a "Begin the Beguine" if Cole Porter had not had the leisure and the means to travel.

For travel took him to exotic places, provided him with fresh experiences, and it was out of these that much of his melody grew. In Morocco, for instance, he heard a Mohammedan priest calling the faithful to worship with that weird wail which can be heard throughout the Middle East. And according to Porter's own account, that was the inspiration for "Night and Day." If you listen, you can hear it in the insistent monotone and the strange harmonies of the song.

Later, in the Lesser Sunda Islands, the restless, eager Porter saw a native dance. Completely beguiled by its pulsating rhythm, he turned his experience into a fine piece of music— "Begin the Beguine." It is doubtful whether he could have written it in Tin Pan Alley.

Others of his works, more American in flavor, nevertheless derived a certain freshness of viewpoint from his wanderings. He wrote the entire score of *Anything Goes,* for instance, while cruising lazily down the Rhine in Germany.

Most of Porter's most characteristic songs have a touch of the exotic—a certain foreign quality which sets them apart. But he always brings to them some of the Indiana boy which remains in him, a touch of simplicity, optimism, and good cheer to temper the harshness of his off-beat themes.

Whether basking in the sun in Italy or sipping champagne in a Paris drawing room, Porter continued to write. He has the happy facility of being able to compose without pencil or paper and in the midst of the most chaotic babble. Slumped in a chair with his hands over his eyes, he will work out a whole song—both words and music—in his head, while the party goes on. Then when he gets a chance he simply sets it down on manuscript paper or dictates it to a musical secretary.

He usually starts with a title, figures out a climax or "punch" line (usually near the end), and then works backward to the beginning. He says that he does his best work lying on his back looking at the ceiling, but ideas come to him most frequently when he is shaving, dressing, or being driven in an automobile. Crowds do not bother him—in fact, parties stimulate his mind.

So it is not surprising that he has managed to turn out so many musical comedies while apparently doing nothing more serious than twiddling his thumbs. After *Hitchy Koo* and the *Greenwich Village Follies of 1924,* he did not have another Broadway hit until *Paris* in 1929. That same year he did *Fifty Million Frenchmen,* and his reputation was secure.

Then followed *The New Yorkers* (1930), which featured Jimmy Durante; *Gay Divorce* (1932), in which "Night and Day" was first heard; *Anything Goes* (1934), with Victor Moore and Ethel Merman; *Jubilee* (1935), which introduced "Begin the Beguine"; and *Red Hot and Blue* (1936), in which Bob Hope sang "It's DeLovely" with Ethel Merman.

Then, in 1937, his career was threatened by a serious accident. He had always loved horses and riding. One day, while he was riding with friends on Long Island, his horse faltered. Porter was thrown and the horse fell on him, inflicting compound fractures of both legs.

Now the restless, active composer, who feared boredom more than anything else in life, was faced with hospitalization and long months of recuperation. In order that he might walk again, he underwent more than thirty painful operations on his legs. In addition to the physical strain, the enforced inactivity was very hard on Porter.

Finally his doctor advised him to go back to work, even though he was still under drugs to relieve the pain. Although he could not yet walk with a cane and was forced to use a wheel chair, the doctor said: "Travel." Porter did both. In fact, he was still on crutches and in considerable physical torment when he wrote the score for *Leave It to Me.*

This show, which was produced in 1938, featured Victor Moore, Sophie Tucker, and William Gaxton—all old dependable standbys of the musical comedy stage. But the chief debt owed to it by the American public was the introduction of a young unknown named Mary Martin. In this Cole Porter musical she got her big break, and the public has been getting them ever since.

In 1939 came *DuBarry Was A Lady.* The clowning of Ethel Merman and Bert Lahr and the hilarious song, "Friendship," were almost overshadowed by Broadway's discovery of Betty Grable. She had been a Hollywood bit player for years until she came East to do a real musical. After *DuBarry* she was a star.

Let's Face It (1941) featured Danny Kaye, who, up to then, had been known chiefly as a night-club entertainer. Although Danny used a great deal of his own material, it can be said that Cole Porter added greatly to his fame with this wartime musical show. *Something for the Boys,* which followed in 1943, was Porter's and Ethel Merman's contribution to wartime morale—he as composer and she as singer of some of the liveliest tunes ever heard.

For the next couple of years, Porter was engaged in two enterprises which should have paid off, but didn't. One was Billy Rose's *The Seven Lively Arts,* for which opening-night customers paid twenty-four dollars a seat and were served champagne at intermissions. Despite a cast of stars and the best writing and producing talents that money could buy, *The Seven Lively Arts* was not a success.

The second venture was *Around the World,* in which the flamboyant Orson Welles attempted to put Jules Verne's story on Broadway. Most reviewers felt that this musical comedy was smothered in production. Too much attention had been given to spectacular stage effects; not enough to book and music.

Now people began to say that Cole Porter was through. He had survived his reputation as a playboy; he had survived painful injuries and a long recuperation; but he could not survive two failures.

How wrong they were was demonstrated when he returned to Broadway with one of the loudest bangs of his entire career. This was *Kiss Me, Kate,* first produced in 1948, and made into a motion picture in 1953. This fresh, lively approach to the Shakespearean story of *The Taming of the Shrew* proved that Cole Porter was quite able to hold his own.

Two of the best songs from this show were "Wunderbar" and "So in Love." In the first of these, it is interesting to note that Porter can make fun of a tune (in this case, an operetta tune), and still make it appealing. He used this same skill in his "Don't Fence Me In," which was written for a motion picture. In this case, he's kidding the Western songs by writing a Western song—and a very pretty Western song it is.

Several of Porter's best songs have been written for the movies, but he is not partial to them. Of all the things he has written, he likes least the score he wrote for *Rosalie,* a film featuring Nelson Eddy and Eleanor Powell. Yet many a Porter fan would include "In the Still of the Night" in any list of favorites.

After *Kiss Me, Kate,* which had a long run both on Broadway and the road, Porter was not heard from for a while. But he was only gathering strength for another assault on Broadway. This came in 1953 with a musical comedy called *Can-Can.* Although most of its players were either European stars or little-known Americans, the show was an immediate success. Soon all of America was singing such songs as "I Love Paris" and *"C'est Magnifique."*

Possibly there was a touch of nostalgia in Porter's score, for he has not lived in Paris since 1939. That back-yard garden probably seemed very appealing from this distance. But it would have to wait, for there was always another musical project in the works.

Before the furore over *Can-Can* had even begun to quiet, Cole Porter completed the score for another musical comedy. This one, with a book by George S. Kaufman, was *Ninotchka,* the screen play in which Greta Garbo and Melvyn Douglas once kidded the Communists.

It's a safe bet that Cole Porter never *will* get around to that hoeing and digging! He's much too busy entertaining himself —and the rest of the world.

KURT WEILL

WE have to thank Adolf Hitler, one of the most vicious men of modern politics, for giving us one of our finest composers. For when Kurt Weill was forced to flee his native Germany and Hitler's storm troopers, the young composer made his way to New York and to a career in musical comedy.

Before his death in 1950, Weill had contributed half a dozen fine scores to the American theater. From any standpoint he earned his place in musical comedy history.

But his story has particular significance to this book, because in a sense it crystallizes the whole concept of foreign contributions to American music.

We are proud of our American music, and justly so. We believe that it has a distinctly native flavor; and this is particularly true of musical comedy songs, which seem to capture the informal charm, wit, and good humor of our land and our people.

But American musical comedy, like almost everything else American, is actually a mixture of many national bloodstreams. In its earliest days, it leaned heavily upon Viennese light opera, and we are happy to acknowledge that debt today. Victor Herbert, with his classical education in the Old World and his gift of Irish melody, introduced a new strain which has come to be regarded as "typically American."

In the melodies of such men as Irving Berlin, George Gershwin, and Jerome Kern, it is possible to detect some of the plaintive melancholy which is the ancestral heritage of the Jews. And Cole Porter's witty lyrics, like those of Lorenz Hart, are comparable with the best of the great Englishman, W. S. Gilbert—the lyric-writing half of the Gilbert and Sullivan team.

We can detect these influences and acknowledge them without in any way detracting from the originality or brightness of the music which these Americans composed. In fact, it is the dash of foreign seasoning that makes the products of the American melting-pot so tasty.

When Kurt Weill came to this country in 1935, he had already made a reputation in his own land—but quite a different sort of reputation from the one he made here. In Germany he was considered one of the young, liberal group, a composer who used music as an intellectual weapon. He wrote operas—comic operas, to be sure, but as different from American musical comedy as steak is from hamburger.

Yet he adapted his talents to the commercial demands of the American theater easily and gracefully, without losing one shred of his integrity or his musical ingenuity. He became a United States citizen in 1943. Had he been spared a few more years of life, he would probably have become as thoroughly American as apple pie.

His musical contributions retained a distinctive quality that no other American composer seemed able to provide, with the possible exception of Leonard Bernstein, who is first and foremost a composer of the more serious forms—*On the Town* and *Wonderful Town* notwithstanding. And at least one of Weill's works, the folk opera, *Down in the Valley,* comes closer to the heart of America than many a native-born composer has been able to reach.

But it is not for these accomplishments that most Americans remember Weill. It is far easier to remember his immortal "September Song," or the haunting "Speak Low." For Weill could write *tunes,* too. You have only to listen to one of his American scores to know that.

This, then, is the story of an immigrant who enriched America—the saga of a sensitive, shy musician hounded out of his own land to find refuge across the sea. It is also the story of how such a man's music, which had all its roots on the other side, became an important part of our American heritage.

Kurt Weill was born in Dessau, Germany, in 1900. Dessau is a small city about seventy miles from Berlin. Since World War II it has been in the Soviet Zone of Occupation, but in Weill's time it was the seat of the Duke of Anhalt. Weill's father, a cantor, encouraged his son's musical leanings; but there was not much money, and Kurt was lucky to be given instructions on the piano by the conductor of the court opera.

By the time the boy was ten, he was earning money as an accompanist. He used to go to the Duke's palace for court musicals, and when the performance was over, Kurt would stay and have tea with the Duke's children. A conscientious objector in World War I, he was even then one of the democratic thinkers who would try to lead Germany out of a wilderness of militarism and political greed.

At seventeen, Weill was supporting his family with his musical earnings. But he wanted to study in Berlin, so, with his father's blessing, he set out for the German capital.

These were dark days in Berlin, and throughout Germany. The defeated nation was filled with poverty and unemployment, seething with political unrest and even anarchy. But there was also a robust artistic movement in Berlin, unafraid of experimentation, anxious to rebuild the shattered world which war had left. Kurt Weill fitted into this nucleus of young intellectuals naturally.

He entered the Berlin Hochschule to study harmony and composition with Krasselt and with Humperdinck, composer of the opera, *Hansel and Gretel.* To support himself while studying, he played the piano in a Berlin beer cellar. Since his income depended on tips, he used to watch the audience carefully, and when he saw someone who looked prosperous being shown to a table, he'd play louder to make sure the newcomer heard him.

It was no way to get rich, but it did provide him with enough money to continue his studies. After his graduation in 1919 he returned to Dessau as voice coach at the opera. Weill, though a small, quiet man, had firm convictions. At his new job he found himself often in conflict with the director of the opera. Since neither of the two men would give in, Weill finally had to resign and move on to an opera house in another province.

Here his first job was to conduct the opera, *Martha.* The conductor's score, however, was being sent on from Dessau, and it did not arrive until the very last moment. Weill took one look and dropped the music, horrified. The score was so badly marked up that he couldn't read it!

Another opera had to be substituted at the last moment. Weill later learned that his antagonist at the Dessau opera had sent him the obliterated score as a last act of revenge.

After a couple of years' experience in the provinces, Weill returned to Berlin in 1921, to study with the great Busoni, himself a concert pianist and an acknowledged master of composition. Weill settled down to the serious business of study and composing, and in time produced a symphony, some chamber music, and other classical forms.

But he had become interested in the stage as a means of reaching the ears—and the minds—of his fellow men without sacrificing seriousness of purpose. He once said that "the musical theater is the highest, most expressive, and the most imaginative form of theater." So it was only natural that eventually he should try his hand at a "comic opera." It was natural, too, that this first work for the stage would be unconventional, bold, and vigorous. *Der Protagonist,* which was produced in Dresden in 1926, was all of these things. It created a sensation in pre-Hitler Germany, not only for the quality of its music and libretto, but for theatrical daring.

On the opening night Weill and a friend, unwilling to face an audience which might prove hostile, disappeared from the theater and missed a total of thirty-five curtain calls! The reluctant composer was finally located and dragged back to the theater where he was pushed onto the stage for ten more. His name was already famous in Germany.

Weill's music was of the sort called "expressionistic" by the critics—perhaps because it did not fit any of the previous classifications for serious music. It was sometimes strident and dissonant, and thus quite "modern"; it combined the jazz of the cabarets with the classical forms of the old masters; and it scorned mere tunes and pretty melodies. It was, in short, the sort of music that had to be listened to, not just heard. And for those who listened, there was great reward in intellectual stimulation, and sometimes in emotional response.

This was exactly the right sort of music for the time and for the place in which it came to life. In a Germany full of ferment and unrest, it expressed some of the potent forces which were still strong enough to speak clearly. When Weill combined his talents with those of another young intellectual, Berthold Brecht, the two produced a masterpiece.

This was *Die Dreigroschenoper* (The Three-Penny Opera), produced in 1928, and an even greater success than *Der Protagonist.* Based on John Gay's *The Beggar's Opera,* which had been a bitter satire of life in eighteenth-century England, Weill's *Die Dreigroschenoper* was called "a flaming indictment of the social evils of its age." It was enormously popular, not only in Germany, but all over Europe. This play was revived in 1954 in a New York off-Broadway theater, with Mrs. Weill (Lotte Lenya) playing her original role.

Weill now realized that the musical theater offered him opportunities no other form of music—not even grand opera—could provide. He decided not to compose for a "limited" audience—limited, as he put it, "not only numerically but emotionally and intellectually." Instead he would try to reach as many persons as he could with his music.

But forces of evil were at work in Germany. Since Weill was a famous man, he was powerful. Since he stood for freedom, moral honesty, and human rights, he was dangerous to the Nazis. Furthermore, he was a Jew. From the day he attained prominence as a composer, Weill was a marked man.

Nevertheless he continued to hurl his defiance at the Nazis, who were growing more powerful every day. In 1930, when he presented a new opera, *The Rise and Fall of the City of Mahogany,* the Nazis started a riot at the theater in Leipzig. Fights broke out in the audience, and the lights had to be kept on throughout the play. The police were called in, and several people were injured.

Oddly enough, the "City of Mahogany" was supposed to be located in the southern United States. Neither Weill nor his librettist had ever been to America. Years later he told a reporter for *The New Yorker* magazine: "You have no idea how little we knew about America. We had read Jack London and we knew absolutely all about your Chicago gangsters, and that was the end. So of course when we did a fantasy, it was about America."

Not even the Leipzig riot could squelch Weill, however. He continued to write musical plays which snapped at the Nazis' heels. In 1933, after Hitler had come to power and publicly announced his dislike of Weill's music, the composer was preparing to open a new show, *Silver Lake*. Late one Saturday night he received a telephoned warning from a friend: his music was to be banned and the Nazis were preparing to arrest him.

He had to move fast. Within a few hours he escaped across the border into France with his wife. He was never to return to his homeland. His parents fled to Palestine. Weill worked in Paris and in London. Eventually he and Mrs. Weill came to the United States, where he was able to start all over again.

Weill was brought to America by Max Reinhardt, one of the great producers of spectacle, for a $600,000 pageant of

Jewish history called *The Eternal Road.* Reinhardt remodeled Oscar Hammerstein's Manhattan Opera House, hired a huge cast (there were no less than 1,772 costumes), and spared no expense to make this the biggest production ever seen in America. Despite all this, and despite Weill's fine score, *The Eternal Road* was a failure. But Weill was not discouraged. He was determined to find a place in this new and strange world.

He went to the studios of the radio stations, he attended popular shows, he journeyed up to Harlem to hear Negro jazz, he interviewed musicians in orchestras. Through all these experiences he was learning not only the language, but the customs and traditions of America. He was also laying a solid background for a career on Broadway. He knew that he would have to aim at popular entertainment, and at a broader audience than he had known in Germany. He concentrated on acquiring a musical style more appropriate to his new environment.

How well he succeeded can be judged by the record. It began with incidental music for Paul Green's play, *Johnny Johnson,* a musical satire on war. But Weill's first really important success in America was *Knickerbocker Holiday,* in 1938.

Knickerbocker Holiday was a witty but good-natured tale of Dutch colonial days in New York, by the distinguished American playwright, Maxwell Anderson. Weill and Anderson met at a party, became friends, and were soon discussing ideas for a musical play. When Anderson suggested the idea for *Knickerbocker Holiday,* Weill was so excited that he sat up all night reading *Father Knickerbocker's History of New York* by Washington Irving.

Anderson has described Weill as "the only indisputable genius I have ever known." While they were working on the new play, Weill showed his great versatility by not only composing the score but also helping out on the book and lyrics, making orchestrations and arrangements, and otherwise doing yeoman's service in the theater.

When the play was ready to cast, the late Walter Huston was asked to take the leading role. For years he had been an important dramatic actor, but few people remembered that he had once been a "song and dance" man. When he accepted the part, Weill sent him a telegram: "What is the range of your voice?"

Huston sent back the following wire from Hollywood: "No range. Regards."

Later Huston asked Weill and Anderson to tune in the Bing Crosby radio show, where he was to appear as guest. He sang one of his old vaudeville numbers in a husky, toneless voice—but both men agreed that there was tremendous appeal in the performance.

Anderson thought it over. "He ought to have something sad to sing, all by himself in the center of the stage." He then disappeared for half an hour and returned with the lyrics to "September Song." Weill composed the music almost as quickly.

The song was a hit in the show, but it did not catch on with the larger public, even when Nelson Eddy played the same role in a movie. However, when Bing Crosby recorded "September Song" in 1946—eight years after its original bow—the song skyrocketed to popularity.

Knickerbocker Holiday set no commercial, long-run records such as those achieved by *Oklahoma!* and *South Pacific,* but it won the respect of most critics and of a considerable, if select, audience. Anderson's book was a powerful argument for democratic government, framed in a pleasantly satirical story. Weill's music still had strong Continental overtones, but it served its American libretto perfectly.

The next Weill hit was *Lady in the Dark,* with a book by Moss Hart. Many critics, and a large part of the theater-going public as well, regard this as Weill's finest American work. The story was a fairly serious one, dealing as it did with psychiatry, but there were dream interludes of song and dance and a liberal helping of humor and wit. Ira Gershwin wrote the lyrics, and when he and Weill got together on "The Saga of Jenny," the laughs flew thick and fast.

The original production, presented in 1941, starred Gertrude Lawrence, who was said to have been paid the queenly salary of $3,500 a week. It also featured Danny Kaye, Victor Mature, and MacDonald Carey. Later a screen production starred Ginger Rogers.

Though few of the songs from *Lady in the Dark* reached hit classification, several of them—including "Jenny" and "My Ship"—are still heard. As one critic pointed out, Weill's "cunningly simplified jazz rhythms and the threatening leer of his jaunty melodies had a peculiar quality of lingering on in the memory of his contemporaries."

In 1944 came *One Touch of Venus,* with music by Weill, lyrics by Ogden Nash, and a book by S. J. Perelman. "Speak Low" was the hit song from this show, but many people prefer to recall Mary Martin singing, "That's Him," or the lilting waltz, "Foolish Heart."

In 1947 Weill wrote two important musicals. One was *Street Scene,* an operatic rendering of Elmer Rice's tragic melodrama. The other was *Down in the Valley*, an American folk opera.

Olin Downes, New York *Times* music critic, called Weill's *Street Scene* "the most important step toward significant American opera yet encountered in the musical theater." Virgil Thompson, of the New York *Herald Tribune,* wrote that Weill was "probably the most original single workman in the whole musical theater, internationally considered, during the last quarter century."

Down in the Valley was an expression of Weill's belief that "the American popular song, growing out of the American folk-music, is the basis of an American musical theater, just as the Italian song was the basis of Italian opera."

Broadway was to see one more Weill production before his untimely death. This was *Lost in the Stars,* based on Alan Paton's moving novel, *Cry, the Beloved Country.* While this musical play was still running, the composer died suddenly.

He had made two careers—one in Germany, and one in America. As Olin Downes put it, he was "a sovereign example of the forces that merge in the American 'melting-pot' toward a national expression."

If you want a vivid idea of how thoroughly American this German refugee had become, you have only to consider the work he was doing at the time of his death. He was planning an opera based on *Huckleberry Finn.*

RICHARD RODGERS

RICHARD RODGERS is none of the things that famous composers are supposed to be.

He's modest—avoids the limelight, keeps out of the gossip columns.

He's happily married—not to an actress or a singer but to a girl whose family he has known since boyhood. He and Mrs. Rodgers are grandparents, and proud of it.

He's as good a businessman as he is a composer. He handles all the business details for the production team of Rodgers and Hammerstein, and his income is estimated at half a million dollars a year.

Of all the many awards and honors which have come to him, he is proudest of the Navy's Distinguished Public Service Award—a non-glamorous, non-theatrical citation which he won for the score of "Victory at Sea," a television film series.

He never starved or really even struggled. He wasn't suddenly smitten with divine inspiration, but has plugged away steadily at music for most of his life. He is, in short, far from Hollywood's idea of a "good story"—but he is a thoroughly professional, thoroughly competent, and exceptionally gifted musician.

Almost everything he has ever written has been for the theater. And all his work has been shared with someone else—Rodgers and Hammerstein, Rodgers and Hart. He is, in the truest sense of the word, a composer of musical comedies.

Two of his shows, *Oklahoma!* and *South Pacific,* won Pulitzer Prizes—a rare distinction for musical comedies, even after Gershwin set the precedent with *Of Thee I Sing*. But what is more important, his songs are as familiar and as well-loved as any in the entire library of operetta and musical comedy.

Maybe part of Dick Rodger's secret is that he never sets out to write a "hit" song. Instead he tries to write a song which will fit a certain mood, a situation in the play, a character in the story. If what comes up turns out to be a hit, Rodgers doesn't complain; but first it must meet the requirements of the show.

That's what happened with such songs as "Oh, What a Beautiful Morning," from *Oklahoma!* and "Some Enchanted Evening," from *South Pacific*. They made the play first, and the Hit Parade later.

This single-minded devotion to the theater is the result of a life-long love affair. Rodgers says that he fell in love with the theater at Saturday matinees when he was a youngster, and he's still stage-struck today. He and Mrs. Rodgers see virtually every production that is presented on Broadway every season.

The nearest he can get to the theater in his family, however, is a grandfather who owned the company that provided the silk that made the tights that covered the legs of the chorus girls in *The Black Crook* (probably the first musical comedy ever seen in America)! His own parents were not theatrical.

His father was a successful New York doctor, and Rodgers was born in Manhattan in 1902. His mother was quite an accomplished pianist, but only as an amateur. She and Dr. Rodgers were enthusiastic stage fans, however, and they used to bring home the entire scores of operettas and musical shows which they saw when Dick was young.

As a result there was always music and singing around the house, and by the time young Rodgers was four years old, he could pick out on the piano simple tunes from such shows as Victor Herbert's *Mlle. Modiste.* With his mother's tutoring and some piano lessons, he was soon able to improvise original melodies. By the time he was fourteen, he had written his first song—a number called "Campfire Days," which he wrote at a summer camp in Maine.

During World War I, while Rodgers was still only a boy, he wrote his first complete musical score. It was for an amateur show put on by a boys' club. The fifteen-year-old composer was a mighty proud lad when he stood up in the ballroom of New York's Plaza Hotel to conduct his own work. It was an auspicious beginning, but actually nothing much came of it—at least not immediately.

A year later Rodgers met Lorenz Hart, and here musical history began to be made. The two young men couldn't have been more different. "Larry" Hart, seven years older, was short, dark, and wiry. He was given to sloppy clothes and unconventional attitudes. Rodgers then, as now, was neat, punctual, and orderly. But for some reason, they clicked together.

They had been introduced by a friend who thought they might like working together. The friend was right. The brilliant, restless Hart and the quiet, able Rodgers began at once to throw off musical sparks, and a series of songs was born. Only one of them eventually saw print. It was "Any Old Place with You," which comedian Lew Fields incorporated in a 1919 show called *A Lonely Romeo.* Rodgers was then only seventeen.

From this modest beginning, the two went on to write other songs—because they loved it, because they had to. When Rodgers entered Columbia, the two worked together on a Varsity Show, though Hart had long since left college. The show was a hit at Columbia—such a hit that some of the songs were adapted for a Broadway show called *The Poor Little Ritz Girl.* Sigmund Romberg also wrote some music for this show.

It is interesting to note that Rodgers also knew Oscar Hammerstein II, who was to collaborate with him many years later, when they were both students at Columbia. But Hammerstein was a senior when Rodgers was a freshman, and the younger man stood in awe. Rodgers recalls that when they met and shook hands, his own hand shook!

Rodgers and Hart had made an impressive first showing on Broadway, and it would be pleasant to record that everything continued to go well for them. Actually it didn't. For five long years they couldn't sell another show or even another song, though they kept trying incessantly. They had to write, so they wrote for benefits, charity shows, worthy causes; but they weren't making any money.

Rodgers meantime had left Columbia and entered the New York Institute of Musical Art (now Juilliard), while Hart was translating and adapting German plays for the American stage. Though they were writing shows in their spare time, it began to look as if their one success would be their only one.

At this point Rodgers was offered a job in the children's underwear business, at fifty dollars a week. He made up his mind to take it, partly because he was discouraged with theatrical business and partly because the friend who offered him the job had already lent him a hundred dollars and Rodgers felt a little guilty. At any rate, he was all set to accept the work when a providential telephone call changed his mind.

The call was an offer for Rodgers and Hart to write the score for a Theater Guild revue. A group of the Guild's younger players had banded together to put on the show, for one night only, to raise money to buy some tapestries for the Guild theater. Even though it was only a one-shot benefit, the power and prestige of the Theater Guild were enough to persuade Rodgers. He turned down the underwear job and set to work with Hart.

Earlier lyricists had been content to settle for trite phrases, worn-out rhymes, and obvious ideas. But not Larry Hart. His flashing wit, his abhorrence of dullness, never let him rest, and he turned out lyrics that were fresh and sprightly. Even his sentimental songs showed an enlightened, intelligent approach to the subject of romance.

And Rodgers' music matched perfectly. Avoiding the tired combinations of notes that had been satisfying Tin Pan Alley for years, he managed to turn out tunes that were singable, hummable, and whistle-able, without ever descending to the level of the obvious and easily predicted melody.

The result was that Rodgers' and Hart's little show for the Guild turned into a smash hit. Broadway welcomed them with open arms, and the one-night benefit ran for six months as *The Garrick Gaieties*! One song from that show is still popular, and in a way it typifies the best of Rodgers and Hart —a fresh mixture of attractive sentiment and witty good humor. The song was "Manhattan."

After the *Gaieties,* Rodgers and Hart were in demand. They had a secure hold on Broadway—a hold which was to last for eighteen years, until Hart's tragic death dissolved the partnership. Then, with Oscar Hammerstein II, Rodgers continued his great work. He was still a young man.

Several years after that first performance of *The Garrick Gaieties,* the two young song writers attended a show at the Guild Theater. The tapestries they had helped to buy were still hanging. Hart whispered to his partner: "Do you realize that we are responsible for those tapestries?"

Rodgers answered: "No. They're responsible for us!"

In 1925 they did another show called *Dearest Enemy,* from which the song "Here in My Arms" still persists. In 1926 came *The Girl Friend,* with its hit song, "Blue Room." But it was not until 1927 that they had another really solid hit show on Broadway.

This was *A Connecticut Yankee,* a musical adaptation of the famous Mark Twain story about a modern-day knight who suddenly finds himself at King Arthur's court. The libretto for the play was by Herbert Fields, son of Lew Fields, the man who had taken their first song.

One never-to-be-forgotten song was heard in *A Connecticut*

Yankee. This was "My Heart Stood Still," and again we are reminded of one of those curious quirks of show business. "My Heart Stood Still," which, for many people, made *A Connecticut Yankee* the great show that it was, was actually composed for another musical a year or so earlier. Fortunately the original show was a London revue, so the song was still fresh and new to Americans when Rodgers and Hart put it in *A Connecticut Yankee.*

Altogether Rodgers and Hart wrote music and lyrics for twenty-seven Broadway shows. It would be pointless to name them all, but a list of some of the songs from these shows is a veritable catalogue of hits.

"With a Song in My Heart" was first heard in 1929; "Dancing on the Ceiling" in 1931. That perennially popular waltz, "Lover," which every so often enjoys a new wave of popularity, came from a 1933 motion picture called *Love Me Tonight.* Other songs from the same score were "Mimi" and "Isn't It Romantic?"

Rodgers and Hart didn't like Hollywood. The composer reported that he would spend weeks working hard on the score for a movie, only to find when the picture came out that the music had either been massacred or cut entirely. He laughs, too, over the fact that Rodgers and Hart got screen credit for Stephen Foster's "Swanee River," because it happened to be included in a score containing songs they wrote for a Bing Crosby movie!

They wrote one song for a Jean Harlow movie, but it was cut out. They reworked it with a new set of words for another film, and again it was cut. Finally they renamed it "Blue Moon," and as an independent song it was one of their biggest hits!

Returning to the stage, they produced such songs as "Where or When," "There's a Small Hotel," and "Bewitched, Bothered and Bewildered." These are only the high spots. There were dozens of others.

Oddly enough, a ballet number which Rodgers wrote for *On Your Toes* in 1936 has been the biggest seller of all. It was "Slaughter on Tenth Avenue," and it is heard frequently today. In the original play, Ray Bolger danced to the music; in a later movie, Gene Kelly. It is primarily an instrumental work, however.

The last musical which Rodgers and Hart did together was *By Jupiter,* in 1942. This show, featuring Ray Bolger, ran for a long time on Broadway. During its run, Hart grew ill, and when he was approached to do the lyrics for *Oklahoma!* he turned the job down. Rodgers went ahead with Oscar Hammerstein II, and the rest is history.

When Hart felt well enough to return to Broadway, he and Rodgers revived *A Connecticut Yankee* with a few added songs. But on opening night Hart disappeared. Three days later he was dead.

Thus ended one of the most brilliant collaborations in the theater—and thus began another. For with *Oklahoma!* Rodgers and Hammerstein formed a new partnership. Although Hammerstein had written great shows with other composers —*Show Boat* with Jerome Kern, *The New Moon* with Sigmund Romberg, and many others—he met his greatest successes teamed with Richard Rodgers.

Although Rodgers' work has been done entirely for the theater and entirely with just two men, the contrasts between his two lyricists are a testimonial to his adaptability. He is considered a very fast composer: Oscar Hammerstein says,

"I give him a lyric and get out of the way." But with Larry Hart, he usually had to complete the whole song before Hart would write a word.

The brilliant and moody Hart was forever putting off work. Once when he was staying with the Rodgers family in the country, he bribed Rodgers' young daughter to hide him in a tree-house so the composer wouldn't force him to write. He loved late hours and slept very little. He did his best work in the wee hours of the morning after an evening spent having fun.

Hammerstein, on the other hand, is almost as businesslike as Rodgers. The work which these two men have produced together is deceptively simple and natural in its effect. Actually it is the result of careful, workmanlike planning and construction.

Rodgers says: "Melodies never come to me; I go to them." When music critic Deems Taylor asked him how long it took him to write "Oh, What a Beautiful Morning" he answered: "How long does it take to play it?" But behind the quick transcription of notes to paper lie months of thought and planning about the kind of song and the kind of mood he wants to create. Then, when Hammerstein hands him the lyric, he can usually fit it to music quickly.

"I cross him up sometimes," he admits with a smile. "I'll give him a waltz when he was expecting a march. But Oscar is always good-natured about it!"

Rodgers was married in 1936. His wife was Dorothy Feiner, whose family had been patients of Dr. Rodgers. Dick had seen her once as a baby. Years later, returning from Europe, he had met her again aboard ship—but now she was a young lady. They were married soon after.

Although Mrs. Rodgers claims that she knows nothing about music, she is an able critic of her husband's songs. When he plays a melody for her, he waits for her response. If she says, "It's very nice, dear," he knows he has to do some more work on it. It's only successful if it gets an emotional response from Mrs. Rodgers. She cried when she heard "Hello, Young Lovers."

Rodgers himself does not profess musical greatness. As a matter of fact, his wife jokes that he will never dance with her because he just doesn't care for music. He never sits down at the piano to play for his own amusement, but he does play for friends. When he hears something which really moves him, he breaks out in goose-pimples.

When he and Hammerstein are working together on a play, they "blueprint" the whole production from start to finish. They know exactly what sort of music and lyrics they are going to provide before they ever set pen to paper. During these blueprint sessions, Rodgers is restless and fidgety. He paces the floor, perches on a chair, gets up again. Hammerstein says, "Dick is a great chair-tester."

Almost everyone around Broadway has heard the story of how Rodgers wrote the music for "Bali Ha'i," from *South Pacific*. He and Hammerstein were having lunch with producer Josh Logan. When Hammerstein showed up with the lyrics (which had been giving him trouble for some time), Rodgers sat down and set them to music in a matter of minutes!

He is said to have composed "June Is Bustin' Out All Over" during a twenty-minute interval while his wife drove their daughter to the movies and returned home. Another time he got a set of lyrics just as he was leaving his apartment. He read them in a cab on the way to a rehearsal, and played the finished melody when he arrived at the theater!

But this facility is deceptive, for Rodgers has given much time and thought to his songs. He is as thorough and painstaking about them as he is about the business details of the producing partnership which he and Hammerstein have formed. In addition to musicals by other composers—Irving Berlin's *Annie Get Your Gun,* for instance—the partners also produce straight comedy and drama. Long after a show has opened and is a proved success, Rodgers carefully watches production details, checks on performances, even supervises the box office, to see whether customers are getting courteous service!

He grows nervous at the openings of his own shows, and always likes to sit near the rear, where he can "run for the nearest exit, if need be." And he has had such good luck opening shows in Boston that he almost never varies. "I wouldn't even open a can of tomatoes except in Boston," he says.

Early in 1954, the two partners set to work on a new show—a musical version of John Steinbeck's *Cannery Row.* This was their seventh musical comedy together. The others were *Oklahoma!, Carousel, Allegro, South Pacific, The King and I,* and *Me and Juliet* (with the exciting "No Other Love" as its hit song). There was also a motion picture, *State Fair,* which is remembered for the songs, "It Might as Well Be Spring," and "It's a Grand Night for Singing."

With such a record of distinguished shows to his credit, Dick Rodgers might have been excused if he sat back and relaxed. But the theater is too much in his blood for that. If there isn't a new song to write, a new play to produce, or a new production difficulty to be worked out, Rodgers will keep busy anyway—interviewing young people who want to get into the theater.

LORENZ HART

THE other half of the team of Rodgers and Hart was the brilliant and moody Lorenz Hart. His unorthodox rhymes, his wit and good humor, and his refreshing approach to sentiment were new to Broadway when they first appeared in 1925. Today they are still untarnished and unspoiled.

Young people of a new generation are learning the words to "Manhattan" and being surprised all over again at their inner rhymes. They're singing "My Heart Stood Still" just as their parents did. They're thrilling to the lyrics of "Where or When" and "With a Song in My Heart." These songs never seem to grow old.

"Larry" Hart, like his partner, Richard Rodgers, was born in New York. He had an older brother, Teddy, who was a famous stage comic. One branch of the family was related to the great German poet, Heinrich Heine, but Larry never made any pretensions to literary greatness.

After public schools in New York, he entered Columbia University, majoring in journalism. He said, however, that he had no desire to be a newspaperman, and that actually he "majored in varsity shows." He often took comedy roles in these student productions. It was in one of these parts that Oscar Hammerstein II recalls first meeting him.

Hart had written a satire on the silent movies and was playing the part of Mary Pickford. As Hammerstein describes it in his foreword to *The Rodgers and Hart Song Book,* Larry "skipped and bounced around the stage like an electrified gnome." He was very short, with a large head and big, dark eyes. Wearing a blonde wig, he was a sight to behold.

Hart seems to have had a ready laugh, and a noisy one. In contrast, the songs he wrote were often subtle, with the humor underplayed.

At Columbia, in addition to varsity shows, he distinguished himself at foreign language studies. When he left college he got into the business of adapting and translating foreign plays for American audiences. It was at this point in his life that he met Richard Rodgers.

Hart never cared much about appearances, and according to reports, the day he met Rodgers he was caring even less. On that occasion he was wearing an undershirt with a checked jacket, dress trousers, and carpet slippers. Only five feet tall, he must have made an unusual picture. But the warmth of his personality and the fun that he sparked and then enjoyed in return always overcame appearances.

Recalling their meeting, Rodgers said: "That afternoon I acquired a career, a partner, and a best friend."

This was in 1918, when Hart was twenty-three and Rodgers sixteen. Rodgers had written a charity show which was six hours long. When he heard of this Hart said: "Cut it to three." Rodgers did, and that was their first collaboration!

Actually the first show they did together was a varsity show for Columbia. Hart, an alumnus, often referred to this as his "post-graduate work." And, he added, it paid better dividends than any post-graduate work he ever heard of.

That first show made enough of an impression to be transplanted to Broadway, as part of the score for *The Poor Little Ritz Girl*. The two young men now considered that they had a bull by the tail, and proceeded to write other musical comedies. The next one was something called *Winkle Town* —which was universally ignored.

One of the songs from *Winkle Town* was the now famous "Manhattan," but for some reason, Broadway producers weren't buying rhymes like "men itch" and "Greenwich," or "Coney" and "boloney." The reason was fairly simple. The times weren't quite right. While America was entering the jazz age, it hadn't yet broken free from the sentiments of the older school of operetta and comic opera. Rodgers and Hart were a step ahead of their time.

During the five years in which they were peddling *Winkle Town* virtually from door to door, they made Broadway only once. With Herbert Fields, a young librettist from a theatrical family, they wrote a play called *The Melody Man*. Since all three men had a hand in it, they used the pseudonym "Herbert Richard Lorenz," made up of their first names.

The disguise didn't help. The play suffered a quick death on Broadway and is remembered today chiefly because it introduced a young juvenile named Fredric March.

Hart was making very little money out of his translating, which he kept up in random fashion. And Rodgers, now through school, was even more concerned with the necessity to be practical. They were ready to call it quits when the

Theater Guild offered them a chance to write the songs for a revue.

This revue turned into *The Garrick Gaieties* and a big hit on Broadway. "Manhattan" was introduced to an audience which was now ready—even eager—to listen. And Rodgers and Hart were made. This was in 1925.

It is interesting to note that there were no less than forty-six musical shows in that Broadway season! Today there are seldom more than fifteen or twenty. But for *The Garrick Gaieties* to have survived in that kind of competition is a tribute to its charm.

According to some critics, a large part of that charm came from the fact that the show was conceived, written, and produced in the spirit of inspired amateurs. But some of this spirit pervaded every Rodgers and Hart show, even after they were established professionals. In 1937, for instance, they did a show called *Babes in Arms,* which featured performers who were mostly teen-age unknowns. One of them was Mitzi Green, then seventeen, who sang "My Funny Valentine." Another was Alfred Drake, who was later to star in *Oklahoma!* and *Kiss Me, Kate.*

When their shows did not celebrate youth, they at least weren't afraid to celebrate new ideas. *Peggy-Ann,* which they wrote in 1926, defied convention by running for the first fifteen minutes without any singing or dancing at all. This, in a day when the musical-comedy opening chorus was almost as sacred a tradition as the box office itself, was revolutionary.

On Your Toes was the first musical comedy to employ serious ballet as a means of advancing the plot, and the unorthodox notion of a ballet about gang warfare was exploited in "Slaughter on Tenth Avenue." *The Boys from Syracuse,* another Rodgers and Hart musical, was the first musical comedy to be based on a play by Shakespeare. The play was, of course, *A Comedy of Errors,* and the comic twin servants were played by Jimmy Savo and Hart's brother Teddy.

Of course neither Rodgers nor Hart can take all the credit for the brilliance of the musical shows they wrote. Often the conception might be someone else's. In the case of *I'd Rather Be Right,* a political satire in which George M. Cohan impersonated President Franklin D. Roosevelt, the book by George S. Kaufman and Moss Hart actually outshone the songs by Rodgers and Larry Hart. And in many of their most successful musical comedies, the play book was by their old friend Herbert Fields.

It was Fields who helped them concoct *A Connecticut Yankee,* for instance. This was one of the biggest theatrical hits the two men ever had. There is an interesting story about the chief song, "My Heart Stood Still," and how it came to be written.

Rodgers and Hart were visiting in Paris soon after their first success on Broadway. Riding in a taxi one night, they were almost hit by another cab. A girl who was with them gasped: "My heart stood still!"

"That's a good title for a song," Larry said.

Rodgers agreed, and they wrote it, for a British revue. When they wanted to use it in *A Connecticut Yankee,* it cost them five thousand dollars to buy back their own song! But the investment paid off.

It was reported that the Duke of Windsor, then Prince of Wales, was particularly fond of this song. He had been invited to the opening of the London revue, and when he attended, he got so much attention that nobody saw much of the show. But he must have heard "My Heart Stood Still," for later, at an outdoor concert, he asked the bandmaster to play it. The harried conductor didn't know the tune, so the Prince obliged by teaching him!

In the 1930's, when depression struck the land, Rodgers and Hart took their turn in Hollywood. For about seven years they were there off and on, writing songs for film musicals. The only one of which they were proud, however, was *Love Me Tonight,* which featured Jeannette MacDonald and Maurice Chevalier—and such unforgettable Rodgers and Hart songs as "Mimi," "Isn't It Romantic?" and "Lover."

Hart was especially scornful of the movies. "No one ever heard of a Hollywood writer," he said. "The fans think the actors make up the dialogue as they go along."

Their first and truest love remained Broadway, and they returned joyfully to contribute ten more musical comedies in the years between 1935 and 1942. Some of Hart's best lyrics were produced in these years: they included "There's a Small Hotel," "Johnny One-Note," "I Married an Angel," "I Didn't Know What Time It Was," and "Bewitched, Bothered and Bewildered." All of them were characterized by the same freshness, the same unwillingness to settle for obvious rhymes and obvious ideas.

At the height of this period a reporter called on Hart in his spacious apartment overlooking Manhattan's Central Park. He had never married. In an attempt to overcome his short stature, he wore built-up shoes and smoked big black cigars. But he was still given to loud ties and unpressed suits.

His chief companion at this time was an aging Chinese

Chow dog called Kiki. He also employed a servant whose duty it was to yank him out of bed. For Hart was given to all-night parties, and not very much given to work.

During the interview Hart recalled that at the opening matinee of the first *Garrick Gaieties,* he stood in the back of the theater with Walter Winchell. When his song, "Manhattan," was performed, he started to leave the theater and had to be restrained. He was sure the show was doomed—the song was "too polysyllabic." But that matinee lasted until seven in the evening! By that time Hart should have known that he was a success.

But in all the years that followed, he never lost his nervous uneasiness. At every opening he would walk up and down behind the audience, muttering when a joke fell dead, and rubbing his hands gleefully if a song went over well. His moods ranged from noisy gaiety to black despair—and they did not necessarily have anything to do with the relative success or failure of his latest show.

There were very few, if any, failures. The nearest was perhaps *Higher and Higher,* in 1940. But even that had its compensations, one of which was the singing of Shirley Ross, who was also a popular motion picture star. There was also a trained seal in the cast, which led Rodgers to comment: "When a trained seal steals the show, you know how bad it is."

But the partners redeemed themselves with their next effort, *Pal Joey.* This bright and unusual musical comedy was based on characters created by famed novelist John O'Hara. And what characters they were! Far from the conventional sweet-faced heroine and sturdy hero of old-fashioned musical shows, these were real-life individuals with more faults than virtues.

But Hart and O'Hara managed to make them, if not likeable, at least unforgettable.

It was in *Pal Joey* that Gene Kelly got his first big break. He had worked his way through the University of Pittsburgh running a dance studio, and had played a role in William Saroyan's *The Time of Your Life*. But in *Pal Joey* he made his name as a dancer, an actor, and a personality.

Also prominent in the cast was Vivienne Segal, who had come all the way from ingénue in an early Romberg show to sophisticated, mature roles such as this one. When *Pal Joey* was successfully revived on Broadway a dozen years after its original production, Miss Segal played the same role—with as much charm and fascination as ever.

O'Hara and Hart must have made a remarkable team, for it is reported that as soon as O'Hara had completed the book and the show went into rehearsal, he went to bed—a place where Larry Hart would have liked to be all along. And it was actually Hart, of all persons, who got him up with an appeal to his friendship for George Abbott, who was staging the show. The hard-boiled, unsentimental Hart pleaded: "You're hurting George's feelings."

Actually Hart was *quite* sentimental. You have only to listen to his love songs to know it. But his avoidance of the standard clichés made him seem at times a rather cynical fellow. Those who knew him best, however, testify that he was big-hearted, sensitive, and fun to be with.

As time wore on, Hart grew more and more elusive when there was work to be done. Rodgers once reported: "It is practically impossible to start him working, but it is a feat of genius to make him stop once he has begun." It used to be necessary virtually to lock him into a room to insure his writing anything. And even then he would often put pencil to paper only when he had the completed score of a song in front of him. If left alone for a moment, he might just disappear.

He was also very much opposed to changing a single word once he had written it; and Rodgers, ever the perfectionist, used to argue with him about this. But the arguments were never personal, and the partners remained close personal friends to the end.

The last show they did together was *By Jupiter,* in 1942. During the writing of this show Hart's health, which had been failing for some time, grew worse, and he entered a hospital. Rodgers took a room next to his, had a piano moved in, and they wrote most of the show right there!

By Jupiter, their twenty-seventh show together, was put together during the early days of World War II. Both their scenic designer and their director were working against the time when they should enter military service. There were less serious, but none the less vexing problems. One of the stars was left without a nurse for her young baby just before the show opened; the male lead proved unsatisfactory and had to be replaced; the cast was battered and bruised from dueling practice. At one rehearsal the leading lady said to star Ray Bolger, "Why don't you stop dancing and take a rest?"

"What's the use?" he answered. "I'll just get tired all over again."

Nevertheless *By Jupiter* finally opened, and was an immediate success. It ran for over a year on Broadway.

While it was still playing, the partners were approached with the idea of doing the songs for *Oklahoma!* But Hart, still tired from his illness, did not warm to the idea. He wanted a long rest, and so turned down the show.

Rumors flew around Broadway that Rodgers and Hart had quarreled. When word came that Rodgers would do the new show with Oscar Hammerstein II, some even accused Rodgers of disloyalty.

There was no truth to any of these rumors. Hart simply could not take on the assignment at the moment, and went to Mexico for his health. Rodgers went ahead with Hammerstein, but there was never any thought of discontinuing the original partnership.

When Hart returned, the two men got together to discuss what their next project would be. They decided that a revival of *A Connecticut Yankee* was in order, and they set to work writing some new songs for it. Their fans had been after them for years to do just this, and in 1943 the revised and revived *Yankee* appeared on Broadway, some sixteen years after its original.

Larry Hart did not live to enjoy its success. The play opened on Wednesday, November 17. He disappeared that night, and despite the best efforts of his friends, including Dick Rodgers, he could not be located. Two days later he was found, more dead than alive, in a hotel room. He was suffering from pneumonia.

Rushed to a hospital, he was given emergency treatment, but did not rally. At that time the drug penicillin, so widely used today in the treatment of pneumonia, was extremely rare. To get some, Mrs. Franklin D. Roosevelt, wife of the wartime President who had been satirized so unmercifully in Hart's show, *I'd Rather Be Right,* interceded personally. But it was too late. Hart was too far gone.

He died during a blackout while Mr. and Mrs. Rodgers kept vigil in a corridor outside his hospital room.

His loss at such an early age—he was 48—was a real tragedy. But the songs he left behind will always be here to remind us of a brilliant and witty young man who believed that it pays to be different. He never studied versification, he never used a rhyming dictionary, he was unconventional in his way of life, his clothes, and his ideas; but he had the genius to turn these qualities into assets.

And perhaps that is something to remember in a time when those who dare to lead have been so seriously challenged by those who follow blindly.

OSCAR HAMMERSTEIN II

HIS grandfather, Oscar Hammerstein I, was a famous impresario. His father, William Hammerstein, was a vaudeville producer. His uncle, Arthur Hammerstein, was a musical comedy producer. His brother, Reginald Hammerstein, is a stage director. His cousin, Elaine Hammerstein, was a silent movie star.

So Oscar II went to Columbia University to study law!

Fortunately, as everybody knows, the theater was so much in his blood there was no escaping it. Oscar Hammerstein II, writer, poet, and lyricist, has helped to provide us with some of the most memorable musical comedies ever produced. With composer Richard Rodgers he has formed a writing-producing partnership that threatens to make the names Rodgers and Hammerstein as immortal as those of Gilbert and Sullivan.

And the theatrical tradition continues in his family. His son, William, is a Hollywood producer. Another son, James, is a stage manager. A daughter, Alice, is a lyric writer. The Hammersteins are here to stay!

It all began with grandfather Oscar Hammerstein, a cigar-maker who emigrated to this country from Berlin, Germany, when he was sixteen. He invented several labor-saving devices for cigar-makers and prospered in the United States. Indeed, he did so well that he was able to indulge his favorite hobby—the theater.

A man of great imagination and courage, he was never afraid to undertake daring ventures. One of these was the building of the Manhattan Opera Company, to compete with the Metropolitan. He introduced Emma Trentini to American audiences in Victor Herbert's *Naughty Marietta.* Such great singers as Mary Garden were among his "discoveries."

The rivalry between the Metropolitan and the Manhattan continued for many years, but Hammerstein was a stubborn man and would not give in. Once, on a bet, he wrote a complete opera in one day. He called it *Kohinoor,* and it was little more than a half-jesting answer to a challenge. To show his utter contempt for the "uptown" snobbery of the Metropolitan, he also wrote a parody called *Faust on Toast.*

The first Oscar Hammerstein built theaters in New York, London, and Philadelphia. He made spectacular failures and just as spectacular comebacks. But before he died he had made solid contributions to the American theater as an impresario and producer of light opera. And it was in the field of light opera and musical comedy that his grandson, Oscar II, was to make his own name.

Oscar the second was born in New York—in what is now Harlem—in 1895. He was named Oscar Greeley Clendenning Hammerstein. The Clendenning after a minister who had married his parents, the Greeley for the minister's wife, a daughter of Horace Greeley.

Oscar's parents had eloped. His father was Jewish. His mother was a Scotch Presbyterian. Oscar II remembers his mother's parents better than he does his father's father, the fabulous Oscar I. Their name was Nimmo, and as a child he spent a great deal of time with them. He was raised as an Episcopalian.

No one in the family wanted young Oscar to enter the theatrical business. His grandfather Oscar considered it too difficult. "There is no limit," he once said, "to the number of people who can stay away from a bad show."

Young Oscar's own father, though a successful manager of several important vaudeville theaters in New York, felt that his son should follow a more solid profession. That was why, when it came time to enter college, Oscar was destined for law.

But the family had reckoned without either Oscar's inherited traits, or his early training. The first show he remembers seeing was an operetta, *The Fisher Maiden,* when he was about four. He used to go to Hammerstein's Victoria Theater every Sunday as a boy, to see vaudeville. Straight drama appealed to him more, however, and he used to cry quite easily. (He still does, he confesses.)

At any rate, it was the most natural thing in the world that when he got to Columbia, Hammerstein should get involved in the varsity shows. He both wrote and acted in them, and it was here that he first met Richard Rodgers, who was to be his partner years later, and Lorenz Hart, who was Rodger's first partner.

In one of these shows, *Home James,* appeared what is

probably Oscar Hammerstein's first song: "Annie McGinnis Pavlova." The song had no lasting value, but it did start Hammerstein on the course he was to follow. The year was 1917, and America was engaged in war in Europe. Young Hammerstein tried to enlist but was turned down because he was underweight.

So he gave up all thought of a career in law and asked his uncle for a job. He wanted to write, and had been encouraged by Carl Van Doren and other members of the English department at Columbia. But Uncle Arthur very wisely made a condition. "I'll give you a job as assistant stage manager," he said, "if you'll promise not to write a word for a year."

Hammerstein agreed, and spent a full year learning stage techniques and studying the theater from backstage. He made copious notes during this time but stuck to his promise not to try to write.

His uncle, Arthur Hammerstein, had been the man to discover Rudolf Friml. As the producer of *The Firefly, Katinka,* and *Rose Marie,* he was responsible for some of the most popular musical shows in history. His all-around experience and wisdom in matters theatrical were of tremendous value to young Oscar during that first year.

Hammerstein recalls having noted a wealth of minor details, such as the fact that it was possible to cover a hole in the sock with a chorus girl's mascara. But trivial or weighty, the things he learned were to become greater treasures as the years passed. Uncle Arthur also introduced him to Otto Harbach, who, as Friml's librettist, was one of the great men in the musical theater.

Hammerstein, in the foreword to his book, *Lyrics by Oscar Hammerstein II,* has described Harbach as "the kindest, most tolerant and wisest man I have ever met." Harbach accepted the young Hammerstein as a collaborator on the books and lyrics of some of his shows—notably *Sunny,* with music by Jerome Kern; *The Desert Song,* Sigmund Romberg's great operetta; and Friml's *Rose Marie.*

But this was later. Hammerstein's first professional play was something called *The Light.* About all that Hammerstein can remember about it was a horrible moment at the opening in New Haven. The heroine was standing in the middle of the stage, speaking the line: "Everything seems to be falling down around me." At that precise moment, her petticoat fell, and Hammerstein fled from the theater!

In those early days, however, Hammerstein was too busy shifting scenery and learning stagecraft to do much writing, even after the year's agreement with his uncle was at an end. Then came the actor's strike in New York, and at last Hammerstein had time to write a musical show. This was *Always You,* with music by Herbert Stothart.

Stothart, who was Arthur Hammerstein's musical director, got such a laugh out of Oscar's script that he roared aloud as he read it. Oscar maintains that this was what sold the musical to his uncle, and thus started him on the career he has enjoyed ever since.

Always You was produced in 1919, and although it was not a particularly memorable show, it was a great success at the time.

Following this satisfactory start, Hammerstein did several shows with Harbach, including, in addition to those mentioned above, Vincent Youmans' *Wildflower.* He learned how to work with composers of many different styles and personalities, but all of them constrained by the same basic requirement—the musical stage.

Hammerstein's belief has always been: "Write for the producer, not the music publisher." In other words, his songs have been tailored to meet the needs of the character, the situation, or the plot with which the play is dealing, and not the superficial requirements of the "hit parade."

The only song he has written which was not for a stage or motion picture production was "The Last Time I Saw Paris." This haunting song, which was set to music by Jerome Kern, stemmed from the headlines of the second World War. Hammerstein was working on a show with Sigmund Romberg when news came that Paris had fallen to the Germans. Hammerstein could not get it out of his mind.

Finally he had to put down in words all the affection and nostalgia and tenderness he felt toward the City of Light. His usual working procedure had been to write words to a tune already composed. But in this case, he wrote the lyric first, and Jerome Kern provided the melody. Introduced by Kate Smith, the song was not only tremendously popular, but had real morale value.

It was with Jerome Kern that Hammerstein wrote one of the greatest musical plays of all time. This was *Show Boat,* based on Edna Ferber's best-selling novel. First produced in 1927, the show made history. It had all the necessary elements for success: a fine story; powerful songs; an excellent cast; a sumptuous production.

But there was something more important about *Show Boat.* For perhaps the first time in history, the musical stage was dealing seriously with some of the same problems the spoken stage had considered: race prejudice, gambling, violence.

True, all of these subjects were within the framework of a highly entertaining plot, but previous producers of musical shows had shunned unpleasantness like the plague. Kern and Hammerstein proved that it wasn't necessary to serve the public with nothing but ice cream and candy. A little red meat was good too.

One of the songs from *Show Boat* is destined to be immortal. It is "Ol' Man River," and just to read its words is to know true poetry. In *Show Boat* Hammerstein found his forte: the creation of lyrics which sound as true to life as spoken dialogue, and which nevertheless have a soaring quality which entitles them to the word "lyric."

There were other fine songs in *Show Boat:* "Only Make Believe," for one, and "Why Do I Love You?" for another. Both of these are still popular. There was also "Just My Bill," with words by P. G. Wodehouse, which the late Helen Morgan sang in the original production.

Once during rehearsals for the show, Miss Morgan needed someone to read lines with her. Hammerstein happened to be present and volunteered. Miss Morgan did not know that he had written the show, or that he already had a solid list of hits behind him. To her he seemed to be merely a sincere and modest young fellow who needed a break.

When the reading was over she turned to the producer and said, "Let's give this nice young man a job in the show."

Hammerstein was grateful for the compliment from one of the greatest musical comedy stars in America.

With Kern, Hammerstein did *Sunny, Music in the Air,* and *Sweet Adeline* as well. Songs from these shows include "I've Told Every Little Star," "The Song Is You," and "Why Was I Born?"—all of which are still popular today.

Kern and Hammerstein worked very well together. Kern

had a keen sense of the dramatic, and Hammerstein, of course, knows a little something about music. Kern is said to have coined a phrase—"the Hammerstein glide"—for the slow edging toward the door which Hammerstein used to begin when he was growing tired of working.

For about ten years, off and on, Hammerstein was in Hollywood. He first went there with Sigmund Romberg, after their successes with *The Desert Song* and *The New Moon.* They were hired by Warner Brothers to make four films, at $200,000 a film.

The experience was a sad one. Only one of these films was in any sense memorable, and that one, only because of a deathless song, "When I Grow Too Old to Dream." Hammerstein tells a funny story about this song. Romberg wrote the melody first—a pensive, moving waltz. When Hammerstein heard it, the words "When I grow too old to dream" popped into his mind. On second thought, they seemed meaningless, but he couldn't get rid of them. It took him three weeks to write the eight-line lyric to this song, and a casual reading would reveal nothing more complicated than a rhyme between "heart" and "part."

Nevertheless the song enjoyed an immediate success, even though the film itself was a dismal failure. Later the publisher asked Hammerstein what the lyric meant. "I haven't the slightest idea!" he confessed.

A later film experience was more pleasant for Hammerstein. With Richard Rodgers he wrote the score for a movie, *State Fair,* which featured Jeanne Crain. One song from this film "It Might as Well Be Spring," won an Academy Award in 1946, and the film itself was praised by public and critics alike.

Hammerstein has taken greater satisfaction from his stage

work, however. One project which came to life in 1943 was an all-Negro, modern-dress version of Bizet's opera, *Carmen.* Produced by Billy Rose, the new musical, *Carmen Jones,* boasted most of the original Bizet music with a new book and lyrics by Oscar Hammerstein II. Spain became North Carolina, the smugglers' den a country club, and the famous "Habanera" was transformed into a rousing "torch song" called "Dat's Love." All of this was done without injuring the spirit or intent of the original. Some critics, as a matter of fact, felt that Hammerstein had improved the opera.

The public loved the show.

But by this time Hammerstein had teamed up with Richard Rodgers when the latter's partner, Lorenz Hart, grew ill. Together they had written *Oklahoma!,* one of the all-time hits of show business. It had been regarded by some as a risky venture, before its opening in New York in March of 1943. The original play, *Green Grow the Lilacs,* by Lynn Riggs, had been no hit on Broadway. There were no big names in the cast. The second World War was in progress. Hammerstein himself hadn't had a big hit for a number of years. And many felt that Larry Hart's refusal of the assignment, and the apparent break-up of the Rodgers-Hart partnership put a blight on the whole project.

It opened in New Haven under the title *Away We Go,* and reports were that it was no world-beater. It dealt with violence and murder (but also with kindness and good humor), and was considered far too unorthodox to succeed.

Nevertheless it was brought into New York without a single change except the title, opened to salvos of applause, and ran for four years. Road show companies are still playing it, and it is revived perennially. It opened up a whole new era in musical comedies, won a Pulitzer Prize, took the Theater Guild out of the red, made stars of Alfred Drake and Celeste Holm, and made about half a million dollars each for Rodgers and Hammerstein.

This was before the sale of movie rights!

Cynics who said they couldn't do it again were confounded when the partners presented *Carousel,* a musical adaptation of Ferenc Molnar's famous play, *Liliom,* in 1945. Featuring such songs as "If I Loved You," and "June Is Bustin' Out All Over," this musical had a long run on Broadway.

Next came *Allegro,* in which Hammerstein confesses "the characters got away from me and wrote their own play," and then the fabulous *South Pacific*. Starring opera basso Ezio Pinza and the lively Mary Martin, *South Pacific* opened in 1949, and ran almost as long as *Oklahoma!*—until early 1954.

One of the best songs from this show is "I'm Gonna Wash That Man Right Out of My Hair." Hammerstein says that it was Mary Martin's own idea to wash her hair on the stage, and so a song had to be written to fit the action. That's how hits are born.

During rehearsals for *South Pacific,* Mary Martin ended her gay and joyous dance after singing "I'm in Love with a Wonderful Guy" by doing cartwheels clear across the stage. One day she misjudged her distance and landed in the orchestra pit on top of the piano. After that, the cartwheels were cut out. The star, even though game for anything, was too valuable to lose.

Following *South Pacific,* Rodgers and Hammerstein wrote two more hits: *The King and I,* a musical adaptation of *Anna and the King of Siam;* and *Me and Juliet,* a story of backstage life. While both these hits were still running, they announced their seventh joint musical comedy—a show based on John Steinbeck's *Cannery Row* characters.

In the meantime they had done one movie, *State Fair,* and as producers, they had sponsored the destinies of several other successful shows including *The Happy Time,* a straight play, and *Annie Get Your Gun,* an Irving Berlin musical.

With Rodgers, Hammerstein enjoys working regular hours, meeting deadlines, and otherwise behaving more like a businessman than a genius. But the details of the producing business he leaves entirely to Rodgers. Says Hammerstein, "He must like it, or he wouldn't be doing it."

Hammerstein and his second wife, Dorothy, live on a farm at Doylestown, Pennsylvania, when they are not in the city. His first marriage, a wartime romance, ended in divorce. The present Mrs. Hammerstein is an interior decorator.

At opening nights of a Hammerstein show, she is almost as nervous as her distinguished husband. He appears calm on the surface, but he perspires so freely that he needs a complete change of clothing by the time the final curtain goes down. Mrs. Hammerstein has given up wearing rings to openings; she kneads her fingers so unmercifully that her hands are all cut and bruised by the time she is through.

Hammerstein does most of his work standing up, to save having to get up out of a chair and pace the floor. He has a specially-built desk with a slanting top for this purpose. He gestures, talks to himself, and ambles about when he's in the throes of creation.

The manner in which he works with Rodgers differs from that which he had fallen into with other composers. He writes the lyrics first, then gives them to Rodgers for setting to melody. Hammerstein always starts out writing in longhand —he says if they were typed, they'd look too perfect and he'd be afraid to make a change.

When he's writing a lyric, he makes up a little tune to hum it to. The melody that Rodgers writes never turns out to have the remotest resemblance to the tune Hammerstein hummed —and Hammerstein says, "It's a good thing!"

After about thirty-six years in show business, with a thousand published songs, forty Broadway plays, and a dozen movies to his credit, Hammerstein could be excused for doing a little reminiscing. That's just what he did in *Me and Juliet*. For the hero of that musical was a youngster who was getting his start in show business as an assistant stage manager.

The resemblance ends there, however. For Oscar Hammerstein, born in Harlem, son of the city and of the theater, spends his happiest hours seventy-five miles away from Broadway at Highland Farm. There, in the second-floor study of a big white stone and timber house, he writes many of his finest lyrics.

As he strolls the quiet acres of rolling farmland or looks in on his herd of Aberdeen Angus cattle, the musical stage seems far away. Perhaps that's why Oscar Hammerstein is so successful at breathing simplicity and freshness into musical comedies.

INDEX

INDEX

INDEX

ABOUT THE AUTHOR

Leonard A. Paris was born in Sheboygan, Wisconsin, but grew up and attended public schools in Muncie, Indiana. He was graduated from DePauw University with an A.B. degree, and he received his M.A. from Northwestern University in 1940.

Because his father and uncle were musical impresarios, Leonard Paris was brought up in an atmosphere of musical shows and operettas. De Koven and Herbert were household names.

For some years Mr. Paris has lived in and around New York. He is at present a public relations manager of TWA, which means that he frequently travels in the United States and abroad.

Just for fun, he plays the piano. And he writes professionally. His articles, fiction, and light verse have been published in *The Atlantic Monthly, The New Yorker, Cosmopolitan, The Saturday Evening Post, Nation's Business,* and many other magazines. It goes without saying that Mr. Paris' secret ambition is to write a musical comedy some day.